Architecture

Architecture
An Invitation

PAUL OLIVER AND
RICHARD HAYWARD

Basil Blackwell

Copyright © Paul Oliver and Richard Hayward 1990

First published 1990

Basil Blackwell Ltd
108 Cowley Road, Oxford, OX4 1JF, UK

Basil Blackwell, Inc.
3 Cambridge Center
Cambridge, Massachusetts 02142, USA

All rights reserved. Except for the quotation of short passages for the purposes of criticism and review, no part of this publication may be reproduced, stored in a retrieval system, or transmitted, in any form or by any means, electronic, mechanical, photocopying, recording or otherwise, without the prior permission of the publisher.

Except in the United States of America, this book is sold subject to the condition that it shall not, by way of trade or otherwise, be lent, re-sold, hired out, or otherwise circulated without the publisher's prior consent in any form of binding or cover other than that in which it is published and without a similar condition including this condition being imposed on the subsequent purchaser.

British Library Cataloguing in Publication Data

A CIP catalogue record for this book is available from the British Library

Library of Congress Cataloging in Publication Data

Oliver, Paul.
Architecture: an invitation/Paul Oliver and Richard Hayward.
p. cm.
ISBN 0–631–16129–5
1. Architecture
2. Architectural practice.
3. Architects-Psychology.
I. Hayward, Richard. II. Title
NA2520.O45 1990
720–dc20 89–17966 CIP

Typset in $11\frac{1}{2}$ on 14 pt Bembo
by Wyvern Typesetting Ltd, Bristol
Printed in Great Britain by
Butler and Tanner Ltd, Frome, Somerset

Contents

	List of Illustrations	vii
	Introduction	1
PART I	ARCHITECTURE FOR ALL	
1	The architecture we live with	11
2	In the vernacular	26
3	The past in the present	37
4	Changing places	48
PART II	ARCHITECTURE AND ARCHITECTS	
5	Making architects	63
6	Creating architecture	78
7	Practising architecture	91
8	Making buildings	105
PART III	ARCHITECTURE FOR TODAY	
9	The rise and fall of modernism	119
10	Architecture on view	132
11	The shrinking world	143
12	Invitation to architecture	154
	Further reading	163
	Index	167

List of illustrations

Greece: Athens, the Erechtheion

England: Oxford, an aerial view

England: Oxford, Radcliffe Square from the north

England: Oxford, Keble College extension by Ahrends, Burton and Koralek

England: the Oxford Ice Rink, by Nicholas Grimshaw

Iran: a central Iranian village

England: a medieval Wealden house, Sussex

Kenya: a traditional Kikuyu compound

Greece: island vernacular, Cyclades

France: Chateau at Chambord, Loire

Mexico: the religious centre of Teotihuacan

France: the Cathedral of Notre Dame, Paris

USA: Pier 39, San Francisco

India: The Hall of the Winds, Jaipur

'Design Guidance': an early example by Raymond Unwin

Germany: Tegel housing, Berlin, by Charles Moore and Associates

Germany: Berlin housing by Hinrich and Inken Baller

Building Typology: nineteenth-century examples

Italy: Nolli's 'New Plan' for Rome

USA: the advance of the skyscraper, New York

Axonometric projection: Wilde Theatre by Levitt Bernstein

Office or studio? Peridot, Oxford

Germany: The Residenz, Wurzburg, by Balthasar Neumann

Proportion: analysis from a 'Liverpool Sketch Book'

Proportion: the 'Golden Section'

Germany: the grand staircase, Wurzburg Residenz

London: Classic revival by Quinlan Terry, Richmond, London

England: building site

England: a computer visualization for an Essex town

Holland: Appeldoorn offices for Centraal Beheer by Hermann Hertzberger

England: London, the 'Crystal Palace' by Joseph Paxton

France: Paris Metro entrance by Hector Guimard

Austria: Post Office building, Vienna, by Otto Wagner

Garden City Movement: Ebenezer Howard's 'three magnets'

Canada: grain silos in Montreal

Germany: AEG turbine factory, Berlin, by Peter Behrens

England: The Red House, Surrey, by Philip Webb

Holland: the Schroeder House, Utrecht, by Gerrit Rietveldt

LIST OF ILLUSTRATIONS

France: apartments, Paris, by Auguste Perret

Switzerland: Goetheanum II, Dornach, by Rudolf Steiner

USA: Kaufmann House ('Falling Water'), Pennsylvania, by Frank Lloyd Wright

France: Notre Dame du Haut, Ronchamp, by Le Corbusier

USA: the 'Climatron' dome, St Louis, by Buckminster Fuller

Italy: Pallazetto della Sport, Rome, by Luigi Nervi

Australia: the Sydney Opera House by Jorn Utzon and Ove Arup

USA: downtown skyline, Austin, Texas

USA: John Hancock Center, Chicago, by Skidmore, Owings and Merrill

USA: New York, the Solomon Guggenheim Museum by Frank Lloyd Wright

Canada: Museum of Anthropology, Vancouver, by Arthur Erickson

Scotland: the Burrell Museum, Glasgow, by Barry Gasson Associates

England: Sainsbury building near Norwich, by Norman Foster

France: Centre Pompidou, Paris, by Richard Rogers and Renzo Piano

India: high-rise apartments and squatter housing, Bombay

Turkey: 'gecekondu' self-help housing, Ankara

USA: 'hippy' housing, Sausalito, San Francisco Bay

USA: the Watts Towers, Los Angeles, by Simon Rodia

Kenya: core housing, Nairobi

England: housing in Reading, by BHMS

England: Byker housing, Newcastle upon Tyne, by Ralph Erskine

Introduction

HAVE you noticed that recently there has been more discussion about architecture in the press and on television than there used to be? Not a great deal, it's true, when you consider how large a part buildings play in our lives. Many magazines and frequent regular series on TV are devoted, for example, to the preparation, presentation and consumption of food and wine, but architecture, within which these activities and a multitude of others take place, gets nothing like the same attention. There are specialized journals which are read by members of the architectural profession, but these are not directed to the general public. On the other hand, the occasional radio or TV programmes on aspects of architecture are sometimes unsatisfactory to architects because the issues are inclined to be oversimplified from a professional point of view. Nevertheless, there *are* more features on architecture than there were a few years ago, and that cannot be bad.

It's only when you examine just when this increase in attention to architecture began that doubts arise. For it stems from the time, in 1985, when the proposals for the extension to the National Gallery in London's Trafalgar Square were made public, and in particular, the prize-winning design by the British firm of Ahrends, Burton and Koralek (known simply as 'ABK' to the architectural profession, which rather likes to identify firms by their initials). It was not the design itself that caused the stir; it was a comment on it, likening it to a 'carbuncle on the face of an old friend'. The critic was, of course, His Royal Highness, the Prince of Wales, and such was the effect of his condemnation that the design was abandoned.

Prince Charles's phrase was memorable, if hardly fair; it did not have much basis in architectural criticism but the public in general seems to have been relieved that there was, at last, a champion of its own views and values. We may be justified in asking whether it was the quality of the criticism, or the identity of the critic, that aroused the attention of the media. It would seem that it was more a

INTRODUCTION

reflection of public regard for royalty than of its regard for architecture. But it did serve the purpose of highlighting the important issue of the design of the built environment. Even if the Prince has had no training in architecture he had a serious concern for it, as his subsequent addresses made clear. At the close of 1987 he made a passionate speech at the Mansion House in the City of London, at a function hosted by the City planning committee. He declared:

We *can* make choices about the surroundings in which we live and work. Prosperity and beauty need not exclude one another. If the rules of the planning game are wrong, our democracy enables us to change them. This is a good time to reassert a sense of vision and civilized values.

He was talking particularly about the proposed development of Paternoster Square in the precincts of St Paul's Cathedral, but he made it clear that his words were intended to be widely applicable. Architects were not the sole target this time; his words were as vigorously directed to developers and planning committees.

Prince Charles's choice of a larger target concerns us all. We can always castigate 'architects' as professionals with power to influence design which the layman cannot share. But even if this were true (after all, architects are merely ordinary members of society who have taken a specialist course of training), planning committees and developers are members of society who may have political or financial power but who, in general, have not taken a specialized course in *their* capacity to shape the environment. However such architecture may matter to us, for most people there are many obstructions to exerting any influence upon it.

Most of us are conscious of liking or disliking the appearance of a building, a street or part of a city, and often think of architecture purely in these visual terms. In many cases we are only really aware of other aspects when something goes wrong: when the roof leaks, a room is too hot or unventilated, or when ominous cracks appear in the walls. We may not be sure whether the builder or the architect is responsible for such failures, and probably suspect it is both. What such weaknesses reveal is the fact that building design is concerned with a lot more than appearance, no matter how important that may be. Some of the other aspects are hard to identify, such as the dislike that many of us share for concrete or steel, even when we may feel more secure in a building made of such durable materials. There are buildings that seem welcoming, some that have interiors in which we feel 'at home', and others which, for no easily accountable

INTRODUCTION

reason, we instinctively find unattractive, even hostile. How much can we rely on such emotional responses, and do they change with time and experience?

These are not simple questions, and they have no easy answers. Moreover, we may be able to recognize such reactions to buildings *after* they have been built and we have occupied them – but could we anticipate them when they were sets of plans before a local planning committee? This, after all, is the kind of decision that such a committee has to make, and most of us are probably happier to leave it to them, and save our criticisms till later. Then there is the role of the developer who may be responsible for commissioning and investing in the building in the first place. He (though probably 'he' is a large firm or corporation) wishes to make a profit on the investment, but if people do not respond positively to his proposed development he may be less likely to do so.

We do not have to go far down this path to encounter all sorts of problems, such as the conflict between the appropriate use of public (or private) finance and the needs of the community. New health centres, schools, hypermarkets, housing, office blocks, or sports facilities may be wanted – but what are we prepared to forgo in order to satisfy the demand for one or two of them? Old and much-loved buildings in dire need of restoration may have outlived their usefulness, if not their charm. Do we save them for posterity as part of our heritage, or do we sacrifice them in the interests of the present and future population?

Buildings of an earlier age, we are inclined to believe, are of greater beauty than present ones; somehow, they are *better* than modern buildings. But if we believe this is the case, are we certain that Byzantine buildings are as good as Georgian ones; that Victorian architecture is comparable with that of the early Renaissance, and that a Lakeland farm is the aesthetic equivalent of a Tudor manor house? It's all purely hypothetical of course, because we are considering no specific examples – but any town in Europe (or, for that matter, in New England and, increasingly, in countries all over the world), has to have the means of coping with such problems, and to find the criteria with which to assess its inherited buildings, and to decide whether they should be conserved.

Fortunately, we may feel, most developers go to an architectural firm to put their ideas for a new building in professional hands. Similarly, we turn to architects to advise on the conservation, and sometimes the conversion, of historic buildings from our

INTRODUCTION

architectural heritage. Somehow we expect the architect to have the ability to design a building as modest as a domestic garage or as complex as an airport. It is the architect's job to bring together the countless aspects of the building which have to be considered and to organize them in a coordinated whole. To do so may seem a daunting prospect to the layman, and indeed it is a highly specialized skill, which the architect must acquire in his training.

In spite of the dissatisfaction that some may feel with what is termed, rather vaguely, 'modern architecture', the profession often has an elusive glamour for those outside it. A quick glance through a miscellaneous pile of magazines in a doctor's waiting room will usually reveal a story or two with a 'young architect' as the principal (male) character, even if *Homes and Gardens* or, more rarely, *Country Life* are the nearest that the reading selection gets to architectural discussion. But apart from this rather vague appeal, architects do seem to be the possessors of a great deal of technical and theoretical knowledge which the majority of us simply do not share. They need it for the practice of their profession, we realize, but their conversation is often dense with abbreviations and jargon (all that talk of RSJs and DPCs, CAD and BS numbers, one-offs and articulated spaces) which distance them from so many of the community on whose behalf, directly or indirectly, they design.

Prince Charles's speeches were effective in commanding attention to architecture at least as much because of the uniqueness of his position, as for what he had to say. But for most of his countrymen there is far less access to the media, far less chance of being heard – and, unlike the Prince, they never had the President of the Royal Institute of British Architects to advise them, either. Access to the content of the architectural dialogue is also a problem for most people: the whole subject is complex, and its ramifications are manifold. There are few ways of gaining an entry to it except to become trained as an architect oneself – not a realistic proposition for the majority, though it is a possibility for some. It would seem that the doors to architecture are largely closed. Hence this book, which it is hoped will open one or two of the doors a little, to provide some access to the richness within. It is an invitation to architecture, extended not only to those who are considering taking up architecture as a career, but to anyone who wishes to know a little more about some of the issues that concern the built environment today.

INTRODUCTION

Opening the door

Just what do we mean by 'architecture', and what does the term cover when we use it? Does it refer only to buildings designed by architects; does it extend to all buildings; or is it only applied to some, and if so, what qualifies them to be considered as 'architecture'? These are some of the questions this book will consider first. The relationship of buildings to their sites and to each other, and how they influence the sense of 'place' is an important issue in giving identity to towns and cities. We will consider the user of the building and the significance of personal and public domains, reflecting on the expectations we all have of the buildings we inhabit and use, and the means by which we make them habitable and comfortable.

Apart from the buildings in towns and cities which have often been designed by architects for specific purposes, there is also much rural building which meets the demands of particular functions, even though these buildings were not professionally designed. This 'vernacular' architecture is to be found throughout the world in various forms, though today it is being partially replaced by the growth of suburbs – which some designers do not consider to be architecture. What they frequently *do* accept are the building traditions of our past. In many ways modern design reflects them, but our perception of Western history colours our view of the architecture of other countries. Architecture, it is argued in Part I, is not the prerogative of a few nor the privilege of an elite; it is for all, and by all.

Nevertheless, there have been massive developments in the nature of architecture in the twentieth century which make it unlike any other period. Though there are fundamental physical laws which govern the design of any building, technological innovations and the industrializing of building methods have had profound effects which have created a tension between the aesthetic of architecture and the technology of its production. A number of traditional concepts of architecture have been revised in the process but some principles are seemingly universal, relating to mankind's perceptual and sensory experience.

Knowing about the ways in which people respond to building forms and spaces is a requirement of an architect, part of whose job is to create places that give pleasure. But the practice of architectural design involves much more: the solving of problems related to

INTRODUCTION

technology, materials, economics and three-dimensional organization. Architects are employed to give form and structure to the requirements of a client, but they must also communicate their design ideas to planners, builders and members of other professions through a diversity of media and techniques. And there is increasing interest in architects playing a role as intermediaries, acting on behalf of communities that wish to build. All this requires a specialist professional education, though its nature has changed over the years. Students in schools of architecture are expected to acquire a considerable knowledge of building technology, an ability to think and design spatially and an understanding of the history and theory of their subject. The design studio and some professional office experience are among the traditional ways of learning, but alternative systems of training and practice which recognize future demands on architects have their advocates.

Increasingly, rapid change has characterized the twentieth century and this has been reflected in the international architecture of our times. New theories which accommodated industrialization in building initiated the 'Modern Movement' among architects. 'Functionalism' developed its own aesthetic and its committed exponents created a 'modernist' architecture which was intended to create a new, clean and healthy environment. But disillusion with modernism came in turn, leading to a vigorous critique and the rise of 'postmodernist' theory and practice which is very much with us at present. Such changes raise many questions of taste and fashion in design, and problems of appropriate criteria.

However international these modern tendencies may be, it is none the less true that only a small proportion of the world's population is likely to benefit by them. Around the expanding cities are the vast squatter settlements of the urban poor, living in squalid shanties. They and the refugees from natural and human disasters are the victims of social inequality and grinding inequities of wealth. Such world housing problems present major challenges to designers, architects and planners. We are left with many questions. Does society get the architecture it deserves? How can the layman have access to the architectural debate, and contribute to the making of the environment? On these, and many other issues we hope to offer a few glimpses through the door.

This book is not a condensed history of architecture; neither is it an apology for modern architecture. It is not even a description of what an architect has to do, or an outline of how to choose and instruct one to design a building for you. Nor is it a guide to survival as a student in a school of architecture, or a summary of the examination grades you may need if you are planning on becoming one. There are books on most of these themes, and you will find some suggestions to further reading at the end of the book.

Our purpose is rather to emphasize the issues that arise from such themes as these, and to discuss their importance to all of us in society today. In doing so we have to summarize many aspects of the theory and practice of architecture, and we have to consider how architects are trained and how they go about their job. But we are just as concerned to discuss the involvement of the lay person in the built environment, the person who may not be professionally involved but who is anxious to know more about it and, perhaps, hopes to assist in shaping it.

So our work is brushed in with broad strokes on a wide canvas, or, to change to an appropriate metaphor, it is more a perspective – no, an *axonometric projection* – of the architectural edifice than a set of *working drawings* of its details. (You can turn to chapter 5 to find out what those terms mean.) It is a line drawing of the totality which aims to show how the parts fit together and also to give something of the outside view, the structure and the interior seen with the roof off, and from one viewpoint. But let's not push the metaphor too far; instead, please accept our invitation and let us show you round.

PART I

ARCHITECTURE FOR ALL

CHAPTER 1

The architecture we live with

VERY few people are totally neutral to architecture, though they are not always aware of it. In any group of people one person may be excited by a visit, say for example, to York Minster or St Paul's Cathedral; another may be involved in a dispute with a local authority, perhaps over the siting of a new industrial building complex; still another may be planning to purchase a new house. These are commonplace instances, but in many ways we are all engaged, to a greater or lesser extent, in some aspect of architecture virtually every day. Generally, we have some observation or other to make in the process, though it may not necessarily be expressed in terms of architectural appreciation: the visitor to St Paul's may be searching for the Poet's Corner, or 'listening to the echo' in the Whispering Gallery, the disputant is probably motivated by fear of unwelcome buildings near his home, and the prospective purchaser may be more concerned about escalating prices than the finer points of proportion in design.

No doubt hundreds of visitors to the palaces and country houses that are open to the public go for a 'day out', with the prospect perhaps of a picnic in the grounds, and photographs before the fountains. There would not be a safari park at Woburn, a motor museum at Beaulieu or garden centres at National Trust properties if it was not thought necessary to provide special attractions. Even so, architecture seldom functions solely as a backdrop to these activities (and that *is* a function, even if a modest one); essential to the 'outing' is a tour round the building itself, the culmination of a special day. Even if some visitors go to Montacute or Monticello to soak up the atmosphere and elegance of another age, it is certain that among the thousands who await their turn to see round the châteaux of the Loire like Chambord or Azay-le-Ridaud, there are many who are there solely to enjoy the architecture. You can see them elsewhere, guide-books in hand, studying the finer points of a Vanbrugh palace, a Grinling Gibbons detail or a garden by Humphrey Repton.

Obviously, the numerous visitors to many buildings, from lighthouses to nuclear power plants, are not always motivated by such an aesthetic inquiry, but more by curiosity and the satisfaction of other emotional or intellectual drives. For them, the kitchens, the cellars and the sanitary arrangements are at least as interesting as the banqueting halls and state rooms. Yet all the various responses to the buildings around us are facets of the complex structure of architectural experience. Practitioners and students of architecture clearly have the advantage of specialized knowledge, but the layman's reactions are no less important. Whether they arise, like some of these examples, from the vicarious pleasure of sharing briefly in the domestic surroundings of the privileged few, from a concern about a threat to the urban environment, or simply from self-interest, they are valid because architecture is for all of us. It involves us in a multitude of ways, a fuller understanding of which need not be the sole preserve of those who have been professionally trained. One way of gaining an access to such understanding is to start with a close look at the architecture of our own home town.

A college education

For us, the authors, this means Oxford. 'That's unfair,' we can hear some readers protest, looking around at Barnsley or Butte, 'Oxford is a special case.' Certainly Oxford is richly endowed with historic university buildings while many other towns and cities are not. But, we would argue, *every* town is a special case; no two are alike, and each will have buildings that are unique to it alone. We choose Oxford because it is where we work, and whether in the city or its environs, where we live. It is also where this book is published, by one of the thirty-odd publishers, large and small, whose businesses are located there. This 'sweet City with her dreaming spires' (the phrase was Matthew Arnold's), is where a hundred thousand other people live and work. In the summer though that number seems to double with polyglot crowds of tourists who jostle their way through the streets, or are led in 'crocodiles' round the colleges. What do all these tourists come for, and what do they see?

Up to a point the answer is plain enough: they come to see one of the oldest, and reputedly one of the most beautiful university cities in northern Europe. But to reach it, and the architecture of the city itself, the visitor has to arrive. Probably the most attractive way of doing so, though the least used, is by barge along the Oxford canal, which was built in the early nineteenth century to bring coal to the city. As the barge progresses through that part of Oxford that even pre-dates the university, the open fields of Port Meadows, it is still possible to catch glimpses of the city as it may have appeared in Matthew Arnold's day, with its 'dreaming spires' rising above the red-brick terraces of the formerly working-class suburb of Jericho.

Most visitors to the city today come by rail or coach. The station opens on to a vast and desolate car park. Few cities offer so unprepossessing an introduction. The walk from there is tedious, with a small stretch of riverside walk and the sudden hillock of the eleventh-century 'motte and bailey' castle (closed to visitors) to relieve it. The coach trip from the north from Stratford or Warwick by way of Woodstock is better, bringing one through the Victorian suburb of North Oxford to the great, tree-lined open space of St Giles, the site of the September end-of-harvest fair. Coming from London and the east, the outlying country is more undulating. After the descent from the village of Headington the introduction to the city centre is marked by the roundabout of the Plain with its small pavilion, and the sweep of Magdalen Bridge, with the College to the right. Oxford lies in a broad valley, its limits largely defined by the River Thames (called the Isis by Oxonians), its streams and canal to the west and the River Cherwell to the east. Wedged into this converging maze of waterways the city's growth has been largely restricted, and since the 1930s the Ring Road has been a restraining girdle in all directions. Some of this can be seen by climbing the fourteenth-century tower of the otherwise demolished parish church of St Martin Carfax to gain a view over the city.

Carfax is the off-centre hub of Oxford, on a slight rise where the High Street meets Cornmarket and St Aldate's. Set at knee-height in the wall of a rather dreary former bank building at one corner of Carfax is a stone plaque which reads

This was the Site of Swindlestock Tavern, 1250–1709

It is a reminder that the home town we see is not the town it once was, however venerable many of its buildings may be. By no means all of these are immediately recognizable or accessible; in most cities some are tucked away in back streets which will often retain their ancient and rambling medieval plan. In Oxford, a number of colleges do not open on to the main thoroughfares and urban spaces, but lie south of the High Street. But the general pattern of Oxford colleges is to turn their backs upon the street and to focus on inner courtyards, whose tranquil, regular spaces contrast with the bustle beyond the walls. Customarily, the college apartments are served by stairways ranged around the quadrangles, a dozen student rooms to a staircase. Internal corridors are consequently rare. It is a traditional arrangement that dates back to the fourteenth century.

Many other innovations subsequently influenced the design of the colleges, like the chapels, which largely follow the T-plan first built at Merton, with a choir or chancel meeting a transept or antechapel. Several of the colleges present a fortified appearance, stemming from the times when the students had virtually to defend themselves against riots outside. Embattlements on the college buildings persisted as a decorative feature for centuries after. All the buildings were constructed in local stone from the Headington quarries or, for the details, the finer quality Taynton stone from Burford some twenty miles away. The roofs were usually in slate-stone from the village of Stonesfield. The persistent use of local materials over the centuries has the effect of unifying the architecture of a city or town.

There is a conservatism – or tradition – in design which also has done much to unify it: the widely admired use of fan-vaulting in Oxford for example, makes a lace-like pattern in the stone of the fifteenth-century roof over the presbytery at Christ Church Cathedral, with its virtuoso carving in the pendants. Such vaulting was still being employed in the early eighteenth century in the gatehouse of University College. But a word of caution here; though the Christ Church vaulting clearly inspired John Jackson's roof at Brasenose College chapel in 1659 (for which he was paid an extra £20 for 'his paynes taken about it'), it was constructed in wood and plaster and not in stone. As we may often find, it was both an imitation and an anachronism.

Architecture is full of traps for the casual observer. Take Fellows Quad at Merton College for example, which followed what was, by 1608, the traditional residential pattern on three floors. Built by the master mason John Ackroyd of Halifax, in a late Gothic style which of skilled builders that extended far beyond their own counties, but also the slow assimilation of changing styles in periods of restricted communications. A curious concession to the Renaissance is the great, but superfluous gateway on the south side. Its classical orders rise in succession through four stages, with the topmost level bearing the Royal Coat of Arms of James I and crowned with a diminutive pediment, silhouetted against the sky. The power and influence of both Church and State is very apparent. In turn it was the inspiration for gateways at Wadham College.

History and architecture are inseparable, and it is not possible to understand buildings as we see them today without reference to the succession of influences, new building, alterations, rebuilding and restoration that have taken place over centuries. Sometimes the evidence of the unrealized intentions of a patron and his master mason – we cannot say 'architect' in these cases – can still be seen for us to speculate on what the buildings might have been like. An Oxford example is Christ Church. Its immense Tom Quad was planned in 1525 by Cardinal Thomas Wolsey, who was quite prepared to demolish an ancient priory and three bays of the nave of Oxford Cathedral to satisfy his conception for what he proposed to call 'Cardinal College'. Around Tom Quad can be seen the foundations of the cloisters that he had intended to build, and the springing of the vaults is 'drawn' on the surrounding walls. Unfortunately for the cloisters, but luckily for the survival of the cathedral and the remaining priory buildings, Wolsey fell from power within four years, leaving the project unfinished. The Quad was completed in 1681, but without its cloisters, and Sir Christopher Wren was commissioned to design the entrance gateway. This he did idiosyncratically, if memorably, with an ogee dome on top of a massively proportioned octagonal tower with Gothic details.

Professionally designed architecture in Britain really arrived with Wren. Earlier, the buildings were the combined achievements of patrons and master masons, many of whom are unknown to us, like the builders of the parish church of St Mary the Virgin, one of Oxford's dozen churches. Notable for its thirteenth-century tower, with its pinnacled spire, completed in 1320, rising 150 feet above it, the church as we see it today is predominantly in the Perpendicular Gothic style. All the more surprising therefore to find that it has a high Baroque porch with twisted columns and a 'broken and scrolled' pediment, supporting a niche with a shell-shaped head containing the figure of the Virgin and Child. More appropriate in Rome than on a Gothic church (though it even incorporates pinnacles and fan-vaulting), the porch was designed by the felicitously named

Nicholas Stone, a master mason to James I. Revolutionary in its time, it prepared the way for Wren's great Sheldonian Theatre, designed nearly thirty years later in 1664 when the architect was thirty-two years old. The earliest covered auditorium of its kind extant, it has an uninterrupted roof span of 70 feet.

Today, the Sheldonian forms a part of the remarkable sequence of buildings and spaces which includes the Bodleian Library that is widely regarded as one of the finest architectural compositions in Britain: Radcliffe Square. To the west is Brasenose College (named after a curious 'brazen nose' face mask above the main entrance doors), to the east All Souls College and to the south the rear of St Mary's with its fourteenth-century Congregation House. Built at very different times, they once faced a maze of medieval houses, which were demolished after 1714, when a celebrated Oxford physician, John Radcliffe, left an endowment for the building of a new library. The Trustees invited Wren, his successor Nicholas Hawksmoor, John Vanbrugh and James Gibbs to submit designs – rather in the form of a limited competition. Hawksmoor had been producing alternative plans for the whole area, but the symmetry and axiality in which he delighted was somewhat defeated by the irregular placing of the surrounding buildings. He experimented with a drum-like ground floor raised on a plinth, but it was Gibbs who boldly designed the great Radcliffe Camera which now occupies the site, its cylindrical form topped with a huge dome dispensing with the need for axial design. So the professional skills and design sense of Renaissance architects prepared the way for our commitment to architect-designed buildings.

Adjacent to All Souls on the north side, and opposite the Bodleian, is Hertford College. A Hall had stood on the site since 1282, but a new front to Catte Street was built in Palladian style in 1818. Inside the quadrangle is an unexpected projecting staircase, with a Jacobean doorway and a Baroque parapet, though its sweeping, angled spiral recalls the staircase of the château at Blois. From the corner of Catte Street and New College Lane can be seen one of the most photographed of Oxford architectural features, the bridge that links Hertford College with its North Quad, part Venetian Rialto, part Bridge of Sighs. Alas for the snapshot albums, it was built in 1913 to the design of the architect of the staircase and most of Hertford College, Sir Thomas Jackson. Hertford occupied him on and off for forty years, but his eclectic hand is to be seen in substantial ranges at Brasenose, Corpus Christi, Trinity and many other familiar Oxford buildings, from the Examination Schools of 1876 in, as he admitted, 'a sort of Renaissance style' to the Cricket Pavilion in University Parks. With the patina of a century of smoke and traffic fumes much of Jackson's Victorian Oxford, and even of Sir Gilbert Scott's frequently clumsier work, is virtually indistinguishable to the visitor from the architecture of earlier centuries.

Many lessons are to be learned in any city from a study of its historic buildings: the unity that comes from local materials and the meeting of similar design needs, the forces of innovation and tradition in plan, form and details, the impact of external influences and their adaptation to suit new requirements, the processes of building and rebuilding, the evolution and conflicts of styles, the interplay of patron and master craftsman and the eventual emergence of the professional architect, among them. For the casual visitor most of this may be beyond his interest or his knowledge, and it is true that the architecture of a city can be enjoyed without recourse to any historical guides or architectural critiques. But for those who wish to know more about architecture some knowledge of these is essential. After all, no one claimed that access to architecture was *easy*.

Taking a break

Another notice has appeared in Oxford's High Street recently, though this one was chalked on a board rather than incised in stone. It read:

> *Have a break from Historic Oxford. Visit Hologramarama.*

There is, of course, much, much more to 'Historic Oxford' and volumes have been written about it. But Hologramarama? Well, the university for the most part has hardly entered the 'Hi-Tech' Age as far as architecture is concerned, but even so, there is modern architecture to be found. Not much of significance was built between the wars, though by no means all of it was as comically disproportionate as Sir Herbert Baker's shrunken Pantheon of 1929, Rhodes House, or as dull as the New Bodleian Library which terminates Broad Street on one of the prime sites in the city.

In the 1960s a few new colleges and a number of extensions to existing ones were built. The honour of designing the first new college fell to a Danish architect, Arne Jacobsen, noted for his use of elegant proportions and his fine sense of detail. St Catherine's College is situated in a flat meadow by the Cherwell and rather detached from the rest of the university. Jacobsen's plan is relentlessly symmetrical and classical, with hall, library and lecture rooms on the central axis, long residential blocks on the flanks and an 80 foot bell tower at one end. The traditional grouping of student rooms about staircases is acknowledged and the use of yellow facing bricks was perhaps intended to echo the warm stone of the old colleges. A great quadrangle is sketched in the centre, but though it is carefully detailed, 'St Catz' is very cool. The late architectural critic Reyner Banham considered it 'the best motel in Oxford'. Others agreed, if there was a place to put the cars. But the Master of the College, Alan Bullock, has been kinder about the buildings: 'The longer I live in them the more they satisfy me,' he said.

St Catherine's illustrates the problem of inserting modern buildings in a venerable, and venerated environment without recourse to imitation. Wolfson College, designed by Sir Philip Powell and Hidalgo Moya in 1974, is also sited on the Cherwell, still further from the centre. Its massive white forms are relaxed on the river side and seen from across the Cherwell the college settles comfortably in its setting. Like the Great Hall at St Catherine's, the hall at Wolfson is simple but it lacks any feel of special quality, such as the traditional halls can offer. More successful are some of the residential buildings, like the student accommodation at St John's College, designed by the Architect's Co-Partnership as early as 1958. It was virtually the first modern college building and though its serrated contour reflects its unconventional honeycomb plan, it is one of the most effective and enduring. By no means all the new buildings are as good; the horizontal banding of the bleak Sacher Building on Longwall Street which overlooks the gardens of Magdalen College is aggressively incompatible with the narrow, vertical frontages of the Georgian buildings alongside.

As we have seen, one generation can be quite cavalier with its destruction of earlier buildings and in introducing new design innovations. Few in Oxford were as surprising as Keble College, built in 1870 to the design of William Butterfield. Though in plan it was traditional enough, with quadrangles, a sumptuous Great Hall and fine chapel, it was uncompromisingly built in red brick, with polychrome use of bands of stone and coloured brick patterns;

nothing could be further removed from the customary Headington and Cotswold stone, and it offended Oxford taste. So did the 1970s residential building to the rear of the college, designed by Ahrends, Burton and Koralek (ABK). A number of houses were demolished to make room for the fortress-like row. It too was built in brick, but the yellow made no attempt to blend with the college colours. Within, the tinted glass walls are totally unexpected, and the serpentine, glass-covered but partially sunken cloister is as controversial as the original building. Whether the reproduction Georgian of Green College, a contemporary new postgraduate research medical centre on the Woodstock Road which neatly embraces the old Radcliffe Observatory, is the answer to the problem of fitting new buildings into an old environment is a matter of debate; it was built just a shade too soon to be subject to the wittier classical detailing of the postmodern idiom. For most lay observers it is not as radical as ABK's residential block at Keble College, but many architects are disappointed by the lack of commitment to contemporary design which Green College represents.

This gap between the taste of the public, based on what is familiar, and the objectives of architects who must be responsive to the desires of clients and yet feel the need to be at the forefront of knowledge and ideas in their profession, can produce controversial results; in so sensitive an environment as Oxford, perhaps even more so. No building is locally more disliked than the Florey Building, designed for Queen's College by James Stirling in 1971 – and none is more visited by architects, who are keen to see an earlier work by this internationally famous member of their profession. On a branch of the Cherwell it lies like a gargantuan broken potsherd, cast aside by a negligent giant. Defiantly turned away from the rest of Oxford, or the nearby buildings at St Clements, its great bowl is supported by forked concrete props – unbelievably clumsy, or breathtakingly audacious, depending on your point of view. Your view, either way, will be of almost unrelieved cladding in red tiles, as far removed as possible from traditional Cotswold stone. Inside the half bowl, which faces the river, are the students' study bedrooms, as uncomfortably lacking in privacy with their total glazing, as the outside is unwelcoming. Almost adjacent to the entrance is a sign directing visitors to a public car park; explaining to them that the Florey Building is *not* what they are looking for (apart, that is, from Japanese architectural students) has long since ceased to be a joke in St Clements.

ARCHITECTURE FOR ALL

Marmalade and Bull-noses

Though the churches and the colleges have provided the greatest opportunities for new architecture over the centuries, like most cities Oxford comprises a mixture of diverse buildings. Many soon become known to the visitor, especially the museums, of which the Old Ashmolean built on Broad Street in 1683 and hesitantly (but probably erroneously) attributed to Wren, is particularly fine. Its collection was transferred to the 'new' Ashmolean, 200 yards away, designed by an architect–archaeologist, C. R. Cockerell, and completed in 1848. It is a handsome complex in the 'Classical' style, on three sides of a forecourt, the right-hand range housing the Taylorian Institute. Though the side ranges are higher that the central building, the main entrance, with Ionic columns and Grecian portico, is graceful and well proportioned. Just nearby in St Giles is the Martyrs' Memorial of about the same date, designed by George Gilbert Scott in imitation thirteenth-century Gothic style. The 'Battle of the Styles' which they (and Keble) represent, are a reminder that there is nothing new in the heated debate about appropriate architectural design.

Another contributor to this conflict was the University Museum, designed only five years later in 1855 by the winners of a competition, Sir T. Deane and Benjamin Woodward, under the influence of John Ruskin. Ruskin advocated the dignity of the craftsman and Woodward's 'Venetian' Gothic provided numerous stone mullioned windows that could be carved *in situ* by local sculptors. All went well until, it's said, they began to carve less than dignified portraits of university dignitaries; the craftsmen were sacked and even today the façade remains unfinished. The external appearance, Venetian or not, is rather plain and massive in yellow stone; inside though, the contrast is as great as that in the Florey Building, and most would concur, far more agreeable. Groups of slim iron columns support steeply pointed iron arches, bolted yet embellished with witty use of wrought and sheet iron decorations, which hold up a fully glazed roof. It is a confident statement about the new technology of the day, dramatic and unexpected, the frame of the roof echoed by the ribs of the dinosaur skeletons it houses.

Earlier, we planned to break with history, though in Oxford, as in scores of other towns and cities, it is difficult. And that's to be expected, for 'New Towns' are the exception rather than the rule; most places have a historic inheritance into which the newer buildings are inserted, sometimes skilfully, sometimes not. What is noticeable about Oxford when it is compared with other cities is the lack of high-rise buildings: when the spires wake from their reveries they are not assaulted by towering slabs. The building of a 'brutalist' nine-storey block for the Department of Engineering in 1960 sounded the alert, and a height limit on new building was imposed; it did not inhibit the construction in 1970 of the hopper-like Nuclear Physics Lab only a hundred yards or so beyond Keble, but it has protected the skyline to some degree.

Other decisions, past and recent, were not so thoughtful. Take Cornmarket for instance, a short but busy commercial stretch which runs to the Carfax hub. Here there is an ancient church tower and nearby, remarkably, a fourteenth-century shop with other restored shops, adjacent to it. Further along, the courtyard of the Golden Cross Inn, dating from the late fifteenth century, has now been opened to lead into the Covered Market. Across the street stood another much-loved building, the Clarendon Hotel, but this was demolished amidst much vain protest, to make way for a new Woolworth store. Built in 1957 to the design of the then respected architect Sir William Holford it is a large, flat, bland wall of windows framed incongruously in Cotswold stone. Doubtless this was intended to 'relate' to Oxford's tradition, but the building with its open arcade at ground level fails to reflect anything of the scale or form of the other buildings in the street. The old provision merchants, Grimbly Hughes, also fell, to be replaced by Littlewood's. Now, Woolworth's has gone, and this part of Cornmarket has been recently subjected to a 'glitzy' treatment, and opened up as a covered shopping mall, in the fashion of the 1980s.

It links, by way of a couple of narrow lanes, with the Westgate shopping centre and beyond, the multi-storey car park. Standing on the site of old housing along Paradise Street, it belies the name with its massive bulk which incorporates the public library as well as many shops. The shopping mall, which had become the haunt of 'winos' and skateboarders, was recently privatized and given a face-lift. To the chagrin of many designers and architects who deplore the quasi-Victorian details, with globe lamps, bogus mouldings and pastel shades, it has created a far more pleasing environment. Nevertheless, most people prefer the authentically Victorian atmosphere of the old Covered Market (once a butchers' market and still accommodating many of them), even if its timber roof trusses have had to suffer being painted in salmon pink.

In any city, the commercial centre is usually an agglomeration of department stores and high street shops. It has the banks and insurance companies, estate agents and travel agents, post offices and fast-food outlets that other towns of similar size have to meet the needs of their resident populations – without the addition of a university in their midst. There are more bookshops in Oxford than is usual and specialist shops selling anything from academic dress to marmalade are fairly numerous. But those who throng the streets – the daily shoppers from the suburbs and weekend window-gazers from the satellite towns and villages – have little time to spare for architecture; they are too busy negotiating the traffic and dodging the buses. Architecture affects them most at home and at work.

In the past the summer was a hard time for Oxford tradesmen as they awaited the reopening of the colleges on whose custom they largely depended. But the development of large-scale manufacturing industries changed all that. By the mid-nineteenth Century there were three breweries, an iron foundry, a tannery and the University Press among the larger employers, but many more people were employed in service, by the university, in building and in the distributive trades. As least Oxford escaped the worst effects that the collapse of a major industry often caused, though unemployment was still a problem in the 1900s.

It was a local man, William R. Morris, who changed the picture. Beginning by repairing bicycles in his own home, he opened a workshop in Longwall Street in 1902 and started building motor cycles. A dozen years later he was producing automobiles and had bought a Military Training College at Temple Cowley where they could be assembled. During the First World War the expanding Morris labour force was switched to munitions, but when peace was restored car manufacturing thrived. By 1925 Morris Motors had captured over 40 per cent of the expanding British market and had 5,500 employees who kept the popular 'Bull-nosed Morris' rolling off the production line. The Pressed Steel Company making car bodies and later, refrigerators, became very successful and other industries were developed in support. New factories were built, functional if architecturally undistinguished, even spanning the Ring Road. When the road was built it passed through the industrial heart of Cowley to the south of the city. From the perspective of Cowley the university area had become, as one professor wryly observed, Oxford's 'Latin Quarter'.

Oxford United

Most of the people who worked in the industries, who served in the shops, who were employed by the businesses, who built the buildings, repaired the roads, delivered the goods – the people who kept, and still keep, a city flourishing – needed housing. In 1851 there were 12,700 men and women employed in Oxford; a century later there were 60,500. And by 1971 that number had risen to 81,000 – when the total population was still below 110,000. Not all the work force lived in Oxford itself of course, but a large proportion did, their numbers swelled by immigrants and workers and their families from other parts of the country attracted by the job opportunities. You can see this growth reflected in the housing pattern of the city, which has always been constrained by its converging rivers – and the ownership of land.

Close to the canal, which was opened in 1790, are the artisan cottages and working-class terrace housing of the early nineteenth Century. In a single decade from 1821 the housing stock nearly doubled, and at this time the areas of Jericho, Walton Street and St Ebbe's were developed. There was little middle-class housing at first: university dons were obliged to be single and live in college, and the better-off merchants either lived in the city centre or in villas at settlements like Summers Town in pastoral settings a mile or so away. Georgian building largely missed Oxford, the elegantly proportioned houses along Beaumont Street being an exception. In the 1850s the Park Town Estate was built in an Italianate style which was already out of fashion, and it was not until 1860 that St John's College began to develop its lands to the north, between the city and Summers Town – now the suburb of Summertown.

There is a local myth that North Oxford was developed after 1877, when the dons, who were no longer required to be celibate, enthusiastically set about repopulating the city. It's an engaging notion, but in fact, the bulky, neo-Gothic yellow brick residences of the Norham Manor Estate designed by W. Wilkinson were already near completion, soon to be occupied, not by dons but by successful tradesmen. After a scandal over the monopolistic supply of the yellow bricks, many red-brick suburban houses on three or four floors, including large detached mansions and semi-detached villas all with servants' quarters, were built by speculators in the 1880s. At the same time the Oxford Industrial and Provident Building Society built cottages along the canal. With deep gardens and trees lining the streets the North Oxford suburb was leafy and inviting. In the 1960s several of the houses were demolished to make way for student accommodation; belatedly the loss of the Victorian environment was realized and further destruction was inhibited by making it a conservation area. Too large for all but the very affluent today, many houses are used as extensions of the university, as nursing homes, as guest houses, or are divided into student flats. Even the houses of Jericho, once solidly working class, are now being gentrified for sale to aspiring young professionals. Yet, in the several decades prior to these changes the suburb had extended northward to, and even beyond, the Ring Road. Today, it is possible to see the history of comfortable middle-class suburban housing unfold as one proceeds along the Banbury or the Woodstock roads.

Between the World Wars the gaps between the villages of Iffley, Marston, Cowley, Headington and the city itself were largely filled with suburban housing. Some estates were built by the council, many in Headington being well designed and constructed in agreeable red brick with cast stone details. Others were built by private developers, often in the ubiquitous form of the three-bedroomed semi-detached house to be found throughout Britain. In the twenty-five years following 1922 a hundred miles of built-up roads were added to Oxford alone.

Generally, the post-war council houses were simple semis, pebble-dashed, grey and lacking in detail; they were not attractive but they did help solve Oxford's housing problems. These were created partly by the demand from newly arrived workers in the boom years of the 1950s, but there were additional problems arising from the condition of the artisan houses built in the previous century. Many of the residents of Blackbird Leys and other council estates were relocated from St Ebbe's, the area that lies below the Westgate Centre. The narrow streets and tiny houses had been the breeding ground of tuberculosis in the 1930s and the vicar of St Aldate's had been successful in having many of his parishioners evacuated from the area. During the 1960s St Ebbe's was largely 'cleared' (planner's jargon for wholesale demolition) in the interests of public health. Oxford was one of many cities to be subjected to massive post-war redevelopment – but ironically, it was singular in never having been bombed, even though it was treated as if it had been. 'Eastwards of Carfax it will be the old city. Westwards it will be mostly new. The old is very beautiful. We must see that the new is not wholly unworthy of it,' wrote the planner Thomas Sharp in

Architecture, in spite of its condition, can attract large numbers of tourists: crowds gaze at the Erechtheion portal with its caryatid columns in the form of female figures, at the Acropolis, Greece. In the distance below, the modern city of Athens.

View over Oxford. 'Tom Tower' and Christ Church Quad are seen at the left. The High (Street) curves towards Magdalen College. Beyond lie Headington (left) and the Cowley automobile works (right). (Hunting Aerofilms)

The Radcliffe Camera, James Gibbs, 1749. Beyond is St Mary's Church, Brasenose College to the right.

The new extension to Keble College by Ahrends, Burton and Koralek, seen from within the quadrangle. A cloister is enclosed by angled, brown-tinted glazing.

The suspended roof of the Oxford Ice Rink by Nicholas Grimshaw, 1983, showing the masts and sprits which take the tension cables. The rink is sited on the southern perimeter of the city; fields lie beyond.

A village in central Iran, showing the internally focused, private courtyards and almost unbroken external walls. The flat roofs are used for sleeping in hot weather. Some spaces are spanned with domes. Open loggias provide cool, shaded spaces. Walls are of mud and roofs of poles and layers of earth.

The Wealden type of medieval yeoman's house. A central hall extended to the thatched roof; the 'solars', or upper floors at each end are jettied out, with joists exposed. The timber frame stands on a stone plinth and infill is of brick. (Photograph: Richard Francis.)

A traditional Kikuyu compound, Kenya. Dwelling huts are of termite-resistant cedar poles. Deep eaves to the thatched roofs give shade. Storage huts for cereals are raised above ground level.

The Greek island vernacular of cubic forms, whitewashed walls is much admired by architects. House owners may have dwelling rooms on either side of the lanes and indicate their domestic territories by white edging to the stones.

Idealized images of the vernacular are not new. This 'village' was built on the roof of the Château at Chambord on the Loire (begun 1519) for the amusement of aristocratic families.

Teotihuacan, central valley, Mexico. A great religious and urban complex which may have had a population of 100,000, built before AD 400. The Calle de los Muertos (Street of the Dead) extends for two kilometres (right), seen from the Pyramid of the Moon. The Pyramid of the Sun is at the centre of the photo.

The Cathedral of Notre Dame, Paris (begun 1163), seen from across the Seine. The *chevet* or apsidal end of the Cathedral is strengthened by 'flying buttresses'.

Pier 39 on the San Francisco waterfront. An example of urban renewal in a maritime city that capitalizes on the forms of the old commercial port, to provide housing, leisure and retail uses on the waterside.

(*opposite*) The Hall of the Winds, Jaipur, completed in 1768 for the Maharajah Jai Singh's new capital (founded 1728). The 'Hall' is a shallow screen with rooms for the Maharajah's guests to watch the processions in the street below. It was built contemporary with the Wurzburg Residenz and the Radcliffe Camera.

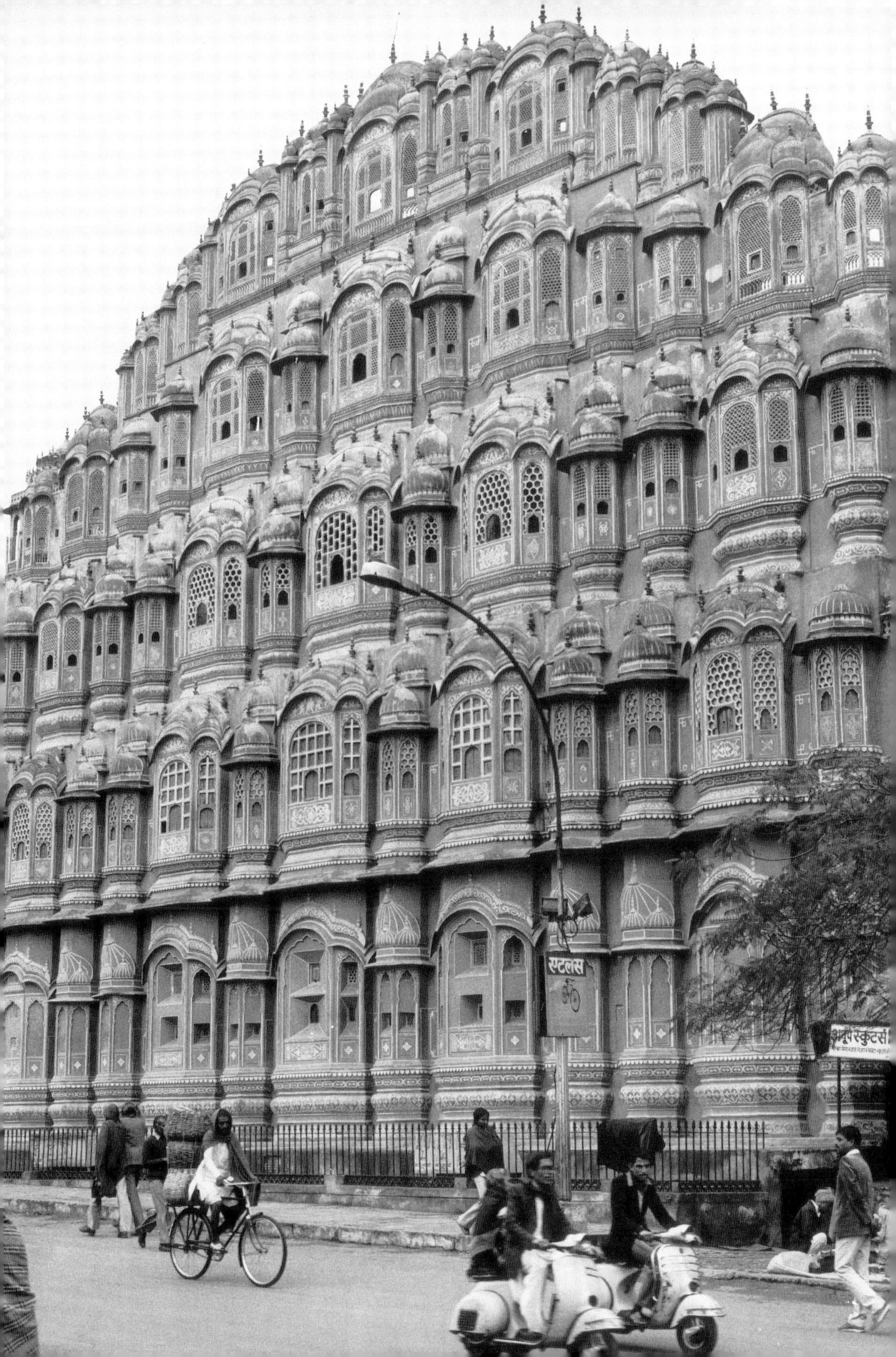
एटलस
अनूपस्कूटर्स

Housing at Berlin's lakeside resort suburb of Tegel, by the American Charles Moore and associates (1985–8). Like most of the IBA housing schemes, the layout provides public access to both sides of the development, sometimes making privacy for residents a problem.

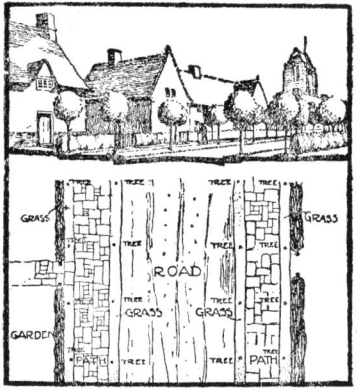

(*left*) An illustration from Raymond Unwin's *Town Planning in Practice* (1909), showing an early attempt at 'design guidance'.

(*right*) Housing on the Fraenkelufer, Luisenstadt, Berlin by Heinrich and Inken Baller (1984). The architects' modernization of the nineteenth-century flats provides a dramatic visual contrast with their expressionist new-build scheme in the background, which is nevertheless accommodated within the same block structure.

1947. Regrettably, his double negative became a triple: much of the new *was* unworthy of 'the old' and by and large, remains so.

The southwest quadrant of the city still suffers from 'planner's blight' – the deterioration that arises from lack of a coherent policy and failure to make decisions. Some new housing, agreeable enough, has been built recently, with a fine prospect of car parks. Here, on the limits of the urban area, where the city leaks out uncertainly to the river meadows beyond, is a large, covered ice skating rink. With its immense membrane of a roof held in tension by steel cables which stretch from masts to bowsprit and sternsprit, it resembles a great ship temporarily anchored near the cattle pens. To the skaters and ice-hockey teams Nicholas Grimshaw's structure is a pleasure; to many others it is an unwelcome 'hi-tech' intrusion. It does not help define the urban edge, it does not contribute to the street as such, but it brings a note of 1980s technological confidence to Oxford's island of conservatism.

Oxford is the most visited city in England apart from London, and so the chances are rather higher that you have been to it already, or will visit it in the future. People come to Oxford largely because of its architecture and it is extremely fortunate, if we are to take Oxford as an example, that it has so many buildings of distinction within its limits. We, the authors, are lucky that we are able to use our home city to exemplify the range of historical and current architectural issues which the inheritance of the past, and the design ideas of the present, inevitably raise. But *all* Oxford's buildings are relevant to these issues, and not merely those of acknowledged worth. They represent the merits and issues which are to be found in the churches, civic buildings, educational institutions, commercial and recreational buildings, houses and estates of every town or city, the architecture with which we *all* live. In order to emphasize them we have gone into much greater depth here than space will permit in the following chapters. As we explore the wider fields of architecture we may become a little better equipped to confront the history and problems, past solutions and new proposals, of the built environment that we all must protect, share and help create.

CHAPTER 2

In the vernacular

Ask a dozen people what their ideal houses would be like, or get them to tell you about the sort of homes that they would like to retire to, and it is very likely that a number of them will describe a 'cottage in the country' – even one with 'roses round the door'. In Britain the image of the country cottage is an enduring one, though the details may be rather vague. It may be 'half-timbered', or built of 'Cotswold stone', or it may be largely built of red brick and 'tile-hung'. Generally, the details do not matter very much, for to most people it is a dream which is unlikely to become a reality. If they are fortunate enough to be able to afford a 'second home' they may try to find that country cottage, and there is a whole service industry which seeks and markets them, just as there are people who buy and 'do them up' to sell them as holiday or weekend homes. Or if they cannot buy that dream cottage, they can rent one for a couple of weeks in the summer; there is another service industry to provide those too. And if all these options are not available, there is still a cottage garden to look after, in the front of every suburban 'semi' or detached house that proudly bears its half-timbered details.

If you asked the question of a group of people in the United States you might get a different answer; there, perhaps, it would be a log cabin in the woods or beside a lake. And often today, the ideal home may be imagined in the Algarve of southern Portugal, on the Costa del Sol, or some Greek island in the Cyclades. But though the locations may vary, and the buildings may differ, they have a number of things in common: they are hardly ever more than two storeys in height, they have sufficient room to take a small family, they have a self-contained garden or yard, they are situated in the country or a village, they are built of simple materials like stone and timber, and they are 'traditional' to the region in which they may be found. Seldom, except among the very sophisticated or very wealthy, are these 'dream' homes designed by architects. Usually they are modest, 'a little different', even 'picturesque', and though one cottage might look superficially like another they are frequently praised for their 'character'.

So we have the anomaly that some of the most widely appreciated and desired buildings are not designed by architects, and might not even be considered as 'architecture' at all, even though they may seem to have many of the qualities that we would like to find in architect-designed houses. Such local or regional building, often centuries old and constructed by peasants or ordinary folk with no professional involvement in designing or building at all, has been identified by many terms. It has been called, inelegantly and confusingly, 'architecture without architects' – a phrase which awards it the accolade of 'architecture' but which tells us nothing about its nature. Bearing in mind that it is frequently localized and native to the original inhabitants of a region, it is sometimes termed 'indigenous' architecture. It has been called 'traditional' – though this term is often as applicable to any monumental architecture of the past, and in the United States it is often called 'folk building', the equivalent of folk music or folk art. But perhaps the most widely accepted term today is 'vernacular architecture'.

Often, it is argued that 'architecture is a language', and though this is a somewhat abstract idea, it is a persistent one, and we shall be returning to it. For instance, it has been argued that there is a 'grammar' of architectural design, that there is a 'classical language' which designers can use, even that there is a 'vocabulary' of details. If we accept this idea of a formal language 'spoken' by architects through their buildings, then the 'vernacular', the 'language of the common people' as it used to be termed, is the speech of the un-lettered sector of the community. In the days when the majority of our cottage architecture was built the non-literate were also the majority of the population. Though the term 'vernacular architecture' has its critics and its inadequacies, it is probably the most appropriate in general use, and it has been adopted by historians, geographers and environmentalists, as well as architects themselves. So we shall use it.

Vernacular architecture is not to be found solely in the West; on the contrary, it is more evident in the less industrially developed countries, where local traditions in building survive as do hand crafts and skills. This means that we can expect to find vernacular forms in all parts of Africa, Asia and much of Central and South America. It is not always as appreciated in these countries as it often is in the West; in India, for instance, where there are half a million villages mainly comprising vernacular dwellings, the ideal house is more likely to be an urban one, while sophisticated city dwellers have no romantic interest in the rough and insanitary mud houses of the peasantry. It can be argued that vernacular architecture is appreciated most where the tradition of building it has died out. Some specialists in the field contend that the vernacular tradition in Great Britain ended in the 1840s, when industrialized techniques of brickmaking, and the building of the railroads which facilitated the shipment of materials to all parts of the country, together terminated the regional styles.

So what characterizes a vernacular tradition? We have noted some features, such as the fact that it is generally regional or local in nature. Of course, this begs the question 'what is a region?' which may be best answered in the specific cases of each country. However, we can expect to find a number of regions within every country, determined by a variety of factors, such as topography, climate, vegetation, and as far as a cultural tradition like building is concerned, ethnic origin also. A vernacular building type might evolve among a specific group of people sharing, perhaps, language, religious beliefs and social structure which are all reflected in the forms of houses or other structures that they build, or built. Because they were located within their own territory they would generally depend upon locally available materials to make their houses; stone, timber, even grass or hides if these were the most readily available. They would also develop their own ways of assembling their materials to construct the buildings they wanted, and these would be further limited, or extended, by the tools they had developed or were available to them.

Obviously, the kind of building that is comfortable in a hot and dry, dusty climate is not necessarily suitable for a hot but humid one, and neither might be appropriate for a region where temperatures drop to −30°C. In a hot and humid climate, such as one might find in Malaysia or Indonesia, through ventilation which allows the passing of currents of air over the bodies of the occupants is very important. This means that side walls may be made of cane or rattan matting affixed to a strong frame. For many of the Muslim peoples of these regions privacy is a major social constraint on building type, so walls that permit air to pass through them must still screen the occupiers from view. Here we can see how materials, climate and social requirements all interact. When such factors as access to water, pastures and arable land, the availability of markets and communication routes, defence and security in sites and structures are also considered, it soon becomes clear that every settlement of vernacular buildings is really a complex of physical and cultural realities. But in many societies buildings take on levels of meaning and symbolism which are not recognizable, and very seldom respected, by people from other cultures. So perhaps, it is not surprising that the houses of a people of Sudan in Africa, such as the Nuba of the southern Kordofan mountains, are going to be very different from those of say, the Minangkabau of Sumatra or the Sharanahua Amer-Indians on the border between Brazil and Peru.

We may accept that there are major differences between the house types of peoples who live so far apart, in different climes and distant continents. But in fact, one of the delights of vernacular architecture for those who are interested in the diversity of solutions to the problems of accommodating people in buildings, is the variety that may be found within quite small distances. We need go no further than the British Isles to demonstrate this. We find that the 'Cotswold cottage' is built of local stone, and is related to the ways in which sheep were raised in this hilly region, while the stone farmhouses of Devon in which both the farmer's family and his cattle all lived – the family at one end, the livestock at the other – reflect the techniques of moorland farming, as well as the methods of building in intractable granite. We might compare these granite 'longhouses' of West Devon with the 'cob'-walled farmhouses of the east of the county. They are similar in plan form because the method of farming was similar, but they were built in the local material of red clay, called cob. In Dorset we can find stone-built houses too, at the southern end of a limestone belt which swings north through the Cotswolds to the Lincolnshire wolds and the Yorkshire moors. Further east of Dorset the timber-framed houses of Hampshire can be seen, and as we pass through Sussex, with brick-built and tile-hung houses linking with the red brick-clays of Surrey, and the timber frames associated with those of Kent, we can trace each local tradition.

In Kent, for instance, you can find a particularly fine house type which has a central hall the equivalent of two storeys in height. This was a yeoman farmer's house, which had, at either end, a floor inserted to create a 'solar', or upper room where the master of the household could sleep. Because it can be found in parts of Sussex and Surrey as well (for vernacular architecture pays no attention to county boundaries!), it is now termed the 'Wealden type'. It is not the only kind to be found in the area, but it is one of the most striking. There are various ways in which timber buildings in Britain were constructed; the so-called 'half-timbered' house is a 'box-framed' structure with many 'studs', or vertical members between the 'bays', and the walling between them made of wattle and daub (sticks and mud), or later, brick. There are various types of framing, and one, possibly older, form of construction in which pairs of half sections of trees lean towards each other to produce a tent-like profile. These 'crucks' or 'couples' help to support the roof, low walls being built between the pairs. Cruck-framed buildings were constructed over several centuries, and it is possible to find many of them in western England.

There is no need to describe here all the different forms of vernacular house type that are to be found in Britain; there are many, and they are still in the process of being documented by scholars and enthusiasts. If you are interested, there is probably a group doing this sort of work in your own area. And even if the domestic architecture of the past has been recorded, it is unlikely that other vernacular buildings – barns, stables, dove-cotes, ash-houses, to mention just a few – have been studied, measured and compared with others to the same extent. For 'vernacular architecture' may mean many other kinds of building apart from housing. It can include what might be termed 'vernacular technology', the windmills, watermills and other structures which have, or had, a mechanically functional purpose.

It might seem that the whole subject has been neatly parcelled up, docketed and filed away, but that isn't so. In fact, the study of such buildings has barely come of age, and there is a great deal to be learned and understood. It overlaps with historical research, with archaeology, industrial archaeology, geography and many other disciplines and fields of study. It involves techniques that range from measured drawings to dendrochronology (or dating of timber by tree rings). Except for nostalgic collections of photographs and well-meant but hardly rigorous descriptions of these buildings, there was little before the 1960s that seriously recorded and analysed British vernacular. The same is true of many parts of Europe, though in the 1930s 'Open Air Museums' became popular in Scandinavia. In recent years there have been detailed and scholarly accounts of 'l'Habitat Ancien' in France, 'Arquitectura Popular' in Spain, and 'Primitive Architecture' in various parts of the world – terms which are themselves reflections of the positions taken by their authors. In the United States there is a vast literature on the 'log cabins', as they are popularly termed, with innumerable papers on their origins, and the techniques of 'notching' used in their construction.

But though there is far more information now than in the past on the variety of types of vernacular architecture, there are great gaps in our knowledge and a serious lack of coordinated comparative data. Immense areas of Africa, South America and Asia have been very sketchily researched, while the relationship of their buildings to the cultural values of the many societies that build them remains, in many instances, almost totally unknown. Why is this? One reason is that it has simply not been taken seriously, being dismissed as 'primitive' or 'pre-industrial' and therefore irrelevant to contemporary needs. But it is also an indication of the tight boundaries that are drawn around disciplines. Anthropologists, for example, are often in a position to make in-depth studies of peoples and their dwellings, but the nature of their training does not equip them to analyse indigenous architecture. This is a problem for historians and geographers too.

Architects have been more involved in the study of vernacular building than, probably, any other group. Their understanding of structural principles and methods of construction enable them to record and analyse buildings with the skills that they bring to their own designing. But they are not anthropologists and they are generally unaware of the complexities of social structures and value systems that tie the bonds between mankind and his buildings. To be fair, some architects *have* become anthropologists, even to the extent of giving up designing altogether. But they are the exception.

What do architects look for in the vernacular, and why should they be interested in buildings that have not been designed by professionals like themselves? In the first place, of course, they are attracted to them as buildings, as they might be to any other form of architecture: they appreciate them as forms and spaces. Sometimes they recognize in the vernacular confirmation of their own ideas and design philosophies. The celebrated Swiss architect Charles Jeanneret, known as Le Corbusier, greatly admired the 'cubic' forms and whitewashed walls of the village houses of the Greek islands and of the M'Zab, a valley in Algeria. His praise of these houses, which had a number of points of similarity with his own, inspired a generation of young architects to see them – particularly those in Greece – for themselves. But sometimes the qualities that they perceive are not as immediately obvious.

Architects frequently admire the vernacular tradition of an area for its 'integrity', in other words for its capacity to meet the physical, and as far as they are aware, the social needs of a community. They respect the use of indigenous resources, and the fact that local craftsmen who know their peculiarities fashion and assemble them with skill and with 'truth to the materials'. They admire the 'simplicity' of the buildings, by which they do not mean that they are naive or basic, but that they are not designed to impress. Often they praise their 'functionalism', or the fact that there is little in vernacular building that is unnecessary or superfluous. Much local architecture is efficient in terms of the spaces that it offers, and is very often highly appropriate to the prevailing climatic and environmental conditions. Today, it is frequently admired for its relevance to its specific region, especially by architects who are themselves dedicated to 'regionalism'.

It is this essentially local character which has led some architects to think of design with a specific locality specially in mind as being 'in the vernacular'. By this they mean that *any* building that reflects local resources and materials, skills and traditions, is 'speaking' in the 'dialect' of the area. So in their use of the term, a regional architecture designed by local architects and satisfying these conditions is also 'vernacular architecture'. It is a use of the term which is particularly popular in the United States. Just to confuse the picture further, some American writers also refer to shops, chain-stores, filling stations, fast-food premises and many other 'anonymous' buildings on Main Street as 'vernacular architecture'.

Survival in the suburbs

There are some who maintain that the familiar houses of modern suburban developments are the 'new vernacular'. By this they mean that houses in the suburbs are as 'anonymous' as they perceive many traditional vernacular types to be. But while it is evident that the origins of many vernacular traditions are lost in the mists of time, and probably impossible to recover, it is erroneous to assume that pizza parlours, supermarkets, car wash premises, ranch-house developments or chalet bungalows are truly anonymous. It may take a bit more effort than most architects or even social historians are apparently willing to devote to them but the fact is that local libraries, planning offices and company headquarters have enough information for us to identify how, when and by whom such buildings were designed and built. Truth to tell, most architects would prefer that the suburbs did not exist.

The odds are about even that if you are not reading this in a suburban home, you live in one. About half the population of Great Britain lives in the suburbs; the remainder live in the country or in the town. This is the basis of much of the opposition that architects and planners feel for the suburbs. They are wedded to the idea that there should be a clear distinction between 'town' and 'country' (it is not always as clear as to why this should be), and the suburbs, in their view, blur the outlines. Of course, it is certainly true that the growth of the suburbs consumed enormous tracts of rural land, and not only in Britain. In the process some good agricultural land, along with a great deal that was not so good, was turned over to housing, and some of the countryside was lost forever.

Why did the suburbs expand so, and why do they continue to do so? Like any question related to both architecture and planning, the answer is not a simple one. Many factors contributed to their growth and some of these are embedded in social conditions. It has been said that some of the earliest cities known to man, such as Ur, show evidence of suburbs. The cities act as a magnet, and people are drawn to them to share in their prosperity. But whereas the resident of the city proper lives by, or even over, his place of work, those who live in the suburbs generally have to travel to their workplaces by some means. The effect of this is to make the suburbs 'dormitories' without the activities, and some would argue, even the social and leisure life, which make the city appealing. On the other hand, the suburb is perceived as vast and, yes, anonymous, where life is dull and uneventful, and where people can live and die without anyone caring. In the suburb there isn't the sense of identity and belonging that there is in the village, and in (idealized) rural communities. This at least is the myth, and it may be true in some cases. But if you are a suburban reader you may well consider that it isn't true in yours.

If suburbs are an ancient and widely dispersed phenomenon, we may wonder why they promote such invective. The problem began with the Industrial Revolution and the depths of urban squalor which poor, densely packed housing and insanitary living conditions promoted. The poorest people were unable to leave and instead developed their own highly integrated urban cultures, like the Jews in the East End of London, or New York's Lower East Side. (It is a curious fact that cities often have their oldest parts in the east, and expand west.) But as the middle classes grew they either sought houses in prestigious parts of the city or moved out to the suburbs, closer to the country. Soon new suburbs leap-frogged the older ones, and as has often been pointed out by their detractors, distanced them from the rural environment which they liked to have close at hand.

One answer to the 'problems' of city densities and expanding suburbs was the 'Garden City' where people could live within walking distance of their work, yet be in an agreeable, leafy and healthy environment. It was the dream of the planning theorist Ebenezer Howard at the turn of the present century, and a few were actually built: Letchworth and Welwyn in particular. But after the Great War of 1914–18 the campaign for 'homes for heroes' advanced the demolition of the most squalid inner city housing and the building of new suburbs around most of Britain's cities, especially in the south-east, around London. Much of the housing was built under local government auspices – termed disparagingly, 'council housing'. Far more was built by private enterprise, with small builders developing 'housing estates', often on the sites of former, real country estates.

Yet the suburbs could not thrive without transport for, as we have seen, they depend on the central city for the employment of what were termed in the 1930s the 'breadwinners' – who, then, were usually male. Cars were still a leisure luxury, but many families chose to live on the new 'arterial roads' which linked the suburb with town and country. Planners deplored the 'ribbon development' which this encouraged. Most people travelled by train, and the network of the London Underground, even if it did not quite have the abstract logic of Frank Pick's famous map, stretched deep into the suburbs and beyond. Every compartment of a Metropolitan line train had 'Live in Metroland' engraved on its brass door handles or stamped in the thick leather window straps. Commuters stood – and daily still stand – thick on the platforms, to be taken to the city and, ten hours later, to be carried back home again.

Home, more often than not, was a 'semi', the familiar abbreviation for 'semi-detached' (not semi-*attached*, though this would have been more accurate). It was based on a type which had gained popularity in the nineteenth century, with pairs of houses sharing a common central wall. They were cheaper to build than wholly detached houses, and took up less land. But they gave a feeling of independence, and you could get round to the back of the house from the front with ease, which was not the case with the more urban 'terraced' house. It had six or seven bedrooms, sometimes more, in the Edwardian period, but the 'semi' of the housing boom between the two World Wars usually had three bedrooms, a 'living room' (or 'sitting room', or even 'lounge' if you wanted to feel superior), a kitchen and bathroom, sometimes with a separate WC (the initials stood for 'water closet', which was only slightly better a euphemism than 'toilet').

The semi, now an all-electric, or partly electric, partly gas home, suited the new servantless society. It provided levels of comfort, convenience and (near) country living to which most of the population could never have aspired before. And by the time the Second World War broke out a third of the population was living in semis, or, if they were elderly, in bungalows, and if they were 'comfortably off', in detached, but still suburban houses.

Much of the distaste that architects and critics had for the suburban semi centred on its appearance. For the most popular types were strongly reminiscent of English rural vernacular – without being specific enough to be identified precisely with any one tradition within it. There was 'half-timbering' but it was not structural; it was pinned to the outside. There was stone – or rather, stones, millions of them, sprayed as 'pebble-dash' over brick walls. There were gables, tile-hung panels, tiled roofs, sweeping gables, stained glass windows and, front and back, there were countless cottage gardens. But while the occupiers liked, indeed loved, their houses for the associations they conveyed of rural values with the comforts of modern life, architects disliked them for these very reasons. They abhorred the imitation half-timbering and pebble-dash for its 'dishonesty', they hated the clutter of details which failed to have the simplicity of the authentic vernacular, and they objected to the derivation of the gables from old dwellings. Modern living it may be, but the suburban semi did not reflect modern design. Today most architects and planners are still of the same opinion.

Similar criticisms have been made of suburbs in many parts of the world. American suburban houses have been condemned as 'little boxes' made of 'ticky-tacky'; timber framing and plywood panelling is widely used and more perishable than the brick used in British suburban housing. But there is more variety in the plans and animation in the older forms of American suburbs; contemporary 'tract housing' makes more use of repeat designs. The inadequacy of public transport systems has meant that greater importance is placed on mobility by car, which has had profound effects on American highway systems and their links with the suburbs, on urban car parking and the growth of suburban shopping malls and precincts. Inevitably, the immense sprawl of a city like Los Angeles or the rapid growth of a sunbelt city such as Phoenix, Arizona, has been the outcome. Yet suburbs as large are to be found in Australia, Brisbane for example, while Auckland in New Zealand has reputedly the largest metropolitan area in the world.

In spite of forecasts of social catastrophe, wanton crime and the decline of the family, the suburbs have proved to be successful and enduring. Belatedly, they are receiving some recognition and architects who have witnessed the failure of high-rise housing may yet benefit from the lessons to be learned from them, vernacular architecture or not.

CHAPTER 3

The past in the present

MOST of us have 'done' History at school, though the 'periods' that we studied – or suffered – were often very arbitrarily drawn. Remember the significance that was attached to the 'Corn Laws' that somehow defined the end of one period and the beginning of another? Or how European history ended at the outbreak of the Great War in 1914? In some schools 'history' did not even *reach* that date, the span of time considered being determined by regulations from distant authorities and 'Examining Boards'. Then there was 'Geography', no less confusing, which might mean studying 'the Amazon Basin' or it might be a matter of collecting data on population movements for a 'project' in your own district of Peckham or Padstow, depending on the concept of geography currently in vogue.

How often did architecture come into the discussion, even perhaps in the physics lesson in which it could have provided practical examples of structural principles? Very seldom. And if the position was really quite different in *your* school, you were probably more privileged, or at any rate more fortunate, than you would ever have realized. It is usual for 'Architecture' to be 'taught' in the art class, when it is expected to enter the curriculum at all. For isn't architecture 'the mother of the arts' – whatever that might mean?

History and styles

Those art teachers or for that matter, history teachers, who attempted to cope with the subject, blew the dust off 'Banister Fletcher' (the 700-page tome *A History of Architecture on the Comparative Method* was, and still is, generally known by the name of its original author), and dutifully plodded through its chapter on 'English Gothic'. Sometimes the miniscule plans and crowded drawings were hard to follow, even when they were simplified in chalk on the blackboard. It was easier to draw the shapes of windows and doors. Thousands of schoolchildren got their first, and often only, glimpse of architecture through a 'lancet window'.

It was a train-spotter's approach to buildings: recognizing the size and sequence of wheels isn't so very different from learning about architecture by distinguishing between a 'Decorated' window and, confusingly, a 'Perpendicular' one ('Please, Sir; aren't they *all* perpendicular?'). If it is a way of getting into the subject, no doubt it is as good as any other. The trouble is, understanding often stays at this level, with the gathering of details, the counting of cusps and crockets, becoming the total objective. Local history societies do a lot of valuable work, but architecturally, many of their members do not progress beyond what they learned at school. And that, as we have seen, can be very limited indeed.

One of the features of the customary approach to architectural history, whether it has been acquired from school or from the library, is its marked linearity, which is reinforced by the majority of books on the buildings of the past. Whether they are aimed at a popular market or are scholarly works for the more informed reader, they are often ordered on the same ideas that influence the teaching of architectural history. 'Cause and effect' is the usual justification for the linear approach: an architectural innovation inspires its subsequent adoption; what is done 'now' is the outcome of what has been introduced 'before'. And of course this is true; there *is* a chain of causes and their effects in any history, though the causes may be social or climatic, for example, and the effects may be political or demographic. Any of these causes and effects may be incidentally expressed, even if indirectly, in building change (temples may become more impressive, as the priesthood becomes powerful; roofs may be built steeper as precipitation becomes heavier).

Generally though, the relation of cause and effect in architectural history is most frequently discussed in terms of technical change. For one instance among hundreds we might consider the 'flying buttress', whose dramatic form appeared in England at the beginning of the thirteenth century. A good early instance is at the Chapter House of Lincoln Cathedral. When English church roofs were made of timber the stoutly buttressed stone walls were more than equal to the outward thrust that the timber roof exerted. But when stone vaulting over the nave was adopted in Britain from France, the walls at the high, clerestory level were not capable of resisting the thrust. So arches were constructed that extended from the clerestory wall over the side aisles to the outer buttresses, which were made still more substantial to cope with this additional thrust. Even so, there was a tendency to push the buttresses away, and pinnacles were built on top of them to exert a downward force that would transmit the thrust and the weight to the ground. Some splendid examples are to be seen in England, like Henry VII's Chapel at Westminster Abbey, and especially in France, the *chevet* or apsidal end of Notre Dame on the Île de Cité in Paris or the remarkably high flying buttresses at Beauvais being two examples.

It is naive to assume that such an invention appeared almost independently of the anonymous craftsmen who built the cathedrals, following some law of cause and effect, rather than from the deliberations of a master mason seeking to find the solution to a problem, and the skills of the masons working under his direction. Attempts have been made to trace the work of individual craftsmen with some success, though their identities remain elusive. But we know that many travelled as 'journeyman' builders, that they worked from carefully drawn diagrams and were jealous of their trade. Abbots and clerics were clearly open to influence and like designers of any period kept a keen eye on the changes taking place elsewhere in Europe. And they were even susceptible to influences from far beyond. The pointed arch, which is one of the liberating structural innovations which marks the transition from the 'Romanesque' to the 'Gothic', was very probably adopted in northern Europe by masons returning from Syria after the Crusades; it had been used in Islamic architecture since the middle of the eighth century.

When we refer to 'Romanesque' and 'Gothic' we are talking about 'styles', or rather, our interpretation of architectural events which we perceive with the perspective of history. We are so used to these terms that we very rarely question them or consider 'what is Roman in the Romanesque' or 'what did the Goths have to do with the Gothic'? In fact, the term 'Gothic' dates back only to the eighteenth century, and was sometimes used as a derogatory term: 'Gothic' then meant 'German' in origin. As for interpretation, it is remarkable in how many ways the medieval cathedrals could be 'read'. The poet Goethe admired Strasburg Cathedral in the 1770s because it harmonized with nature; fifty years later his countryman Stieglitz was praising it for its expression of the German romantic spirit, among the first of several intepretations in nationalistic or even racial – Celtic – terms. To the architect–engineer Viollet-le-Duc in the 1850s it represented both a reaction against feudalism and the scientific demonstration of functional construction, while early in the present century Wilhelm Worringer declared that the Gothic had nothing to do with beauty, but with psychology: it was feeling expressed in form. Only a few years later Le Corbusier was writing that 'the cathedral is not a work of building art, it is a drama'. Greek 'work' was 'architecture, consisting of prisms, cubes, and cylinders, pyramids or spheres'.

What are we to make of these varied and sometimes conflicting interpretations? We may note that many of these writers had an axe to grind, and that they used architectural form or style as a weapon in their battle for the wider acceptance of a particular ideological position. This means, however, that it is very easy, in architecture as in politics, to be manipulated by persuasive argument. Often there is a moral tone reflected in the criticism which is frequently present in architectural history, and other styles are compared unfavourably with those that are championed by the authors. If there is 'cause and effect' there is also a commitment to 'action and reaction'; style follows style in a succession of architectural developments that reject the forms of their predecessors.

Customarily, the progression makes a concession to 'the primitive hut', and nods towards Stonehenge and other mystic sites before embarking on architecture 'proper'. This means Egypt: its prehistoric, Ancient (for example, the Pyramids of Gizeh), Middle and New Empires (Thebes, Abu Simbel), through the periods of Persian, Greek and Roman domination, spanning some 5000 years and nearly thirty dynasties. Much of this immense period – a hundred times the life of 'modernist' architecture – overlaps the Chaldean (Ur, Babylon), Assyrian (Nineveh) and Persian (Persepolis) cultures which succeeded each other over four millennia. Yet for half of that time, from approximately 2000 BC, in eastern Mediterranean sites in Turkey (Hattusas, Hittite), the islands (Knossos, Crete), and mainland Greece (Mycenae) Bronze Age cities flourished. After the eruption of the volcano of Santorini brought about the destruction of the Cretan palaces the habitual sequence moves to the Dorian occupation of Greece and the consolidation of the Greek commonwealth in the sixth century BC, with Athens as its centre of empire.

It isn't necessary to continue this progression through the stages of Greek, Roman, early Christian and Byzantine architecture yet again. The point is that it is essentially a familiar technique which strings the styles like beads on the thread of a linear history. There is plenty of justification for this narrative but, as we have briefly noted, it tends to minimize the contemporary nature of many architectural traditions. There is a common tendency to present an account of history which leads, seemingly inevitably, to the development of architecture in the West, and ultimately to the 'Modern Movement'; a succession which accommodates or ignores other architectural traditions if they do not support this interpretation. North Africa, Asia Minor and Persia are considered as significant enough in the evolution of 'Western' civilization to be incorporated without question into the architectural lineage in the sequence we have summarized; but it is rare for them to appear again except as virtual footnotes to the unfolding story.

In much the same way, the architecture of Russia, or the Balkans and Eastern Europe, and even of Scandinavia is played down, as if there was little of importance except such aberrations as the 'stave churches' of Norway, the 'onion' domes of the Kremlin, or the Baroque exuberance of the Zwinger palace in Dresden. Such 'exceptions' seem to confirm an unstated rule – that architecture reached its peaks of achievement in Western Europe. This ethnocentrism – for that is what it is, a belief that the world revolves around where *we* are – has coloured our attitudes to the architectural achievements of cultures beyond our immediate horizons.

Take, for example, that embarrassing gap in the history of Western architecture when nothing very much happened: the *500 years* or so between the completion of Haghia Sophia in Constantinople (Istanbul), in AD 536, and the commencement of St Mark's in Venice in 1042. This was a span of centuries which was rich in architecture in other parts of the world. Long before the *conquistadores* of Spain and Portugal ruthlessly and systematically destroyed them or their successors, cultures whose growth and development paralleled those of Greece and Rome were still flourishing in Middle America: the great temple complex of Teotihuacan in Central Mexico, and the vertiginous pyramids of the great plaza of Tikal in Peten, or the no less imposing religious sites of Chichen Itza in Yucatan, among them. In South America, the Nazca on the south coast of Peru – noted now for their immense symbolic creatures etched on the desert floor – were still powerful. Meanwhile, in the valleys of the southern highlands the Tiahuanaco

ARCHITECTURE FOR ALL

expanded their empire with planned cities and irrigation canal systems.

Far to the east, this was the period of the supremacy of the T'ang Dynasty in China, though regrettably, very little survives of its capital Ch'ang-an, then the largest and finest city in the world. Ch'ang-an, however, was the inspiration for the planning in AD 708 of the Japanese capital of Nara and, eighty years later, of Heian-kyo (Kyoto), which was to be the imperial capital for a thousand years. Nara's elegant temples, like Toshodaiji Kondo and the immense timber Buddha Hall of the Todaiji monastery, have the tranquillity and sophistication of a mature culture. But Buddhism inspired many architectural masterpieces and in the eighth century the 'nine levels of the cosmic mountain' were built symbolically in the vast geometric complex of stupas – Buddhist shrine mounds – at Barabudur in central Java.

These were the centuries of Muslim expansion when the Dome of the Rock in Jerusalem and the desert mosque at Kairouan in Tunisia were built, and the two-tiered arcades of the mosque in Cordoba constructed. In Cairo at the end of the ninth century the mosque of Ibn Tulun was raised with pointed arches, brick dome and spiral minaret. Here too, a thousand years ago, the world's oldest university was established. Muslim expansion was late in penetrating India and Hinduism was celebrated in the architecture of the shrine city of Bhuvanesvara in Orissa, with its towering ribbed Lingaraja temple. Erotically sculptured and buttressed, the splendid and contemporary Khandariya temple dedicated to Shiva was one of some eighty Hindu and Jain temples which were built at the sacred site of Khajuraho as the new millennium dawned, and Europe awakened to an energetic programme of cathedral building.

Obviously, this is no more than a catalogue of buildings, places and countries, and a highly selective one at that. It does no more than hint at the thousands of other edifices built within the same span of time. But why should we concern ourselves with these structures, so distant in both time and place from ourselves? Surely it is too difficult, and anyway, is it relevant to the understanding of our own architecture, which is hard enough?

Admittedly, it is not easy. The legacy of imperialism and the Eurocentrism of our approach to architectural history hardly help us to assimilate the architecture of other cultures. But we have to live now in a multi-ethnic society; the world can no longer be circumscribed by the limitations of our cultural isolationism. China is the largest and most populous nation in the world; Japan is among the leading industrialized nations, whose values are in many ways far removed from those of the West. India is officially a Hindu state, Islam is the most rapidly expanding religion, which is making deep inroads into Africa. Nations and beliefs are deeply rooted in their pasts. This could be reason enough to study the architecture which so often gives physical form and spatial expression and symbolic meaning to their values.

Apart from this there is much to be learned from the world's architecture which reveals the diversity of man's solutions to the problems of providing shelter, and of organizing settlements in towns and cities. Definitions of territory and systems of defence, means of communication and spanning natural barriers, places for administration and palaces for the centres of power, temples and shrines for the worship of deities, monasteries and schools for those who minister, pavilions and gardens that create order from nature and others built for the contemplation of it, and, most numerous, the dwellings of those who build or use them, and many other kinds of architecture in its broadest sense – these offer profound rewards to the intellect and the spirit. There is much to be learned too, at more technological levels – in the raising of structures, the working of materials, or the spanning of spaces; much to be gained from coming to terms with different concepts of what a building is, or what purposes it serves, and from respect for the skills of craftsmen, or the creative inventiveness of sculptors, painters and gilders. And, at more encompassing scales, we can benefit from the study of the organization of temple and palace complexes, the canons and *sastras* of design principles and urban layout which have created places of mystery or inspiration in societies past and present.

Curiously enough, the first serious history of architecture, *Entwurff einer historischen Architektur*, published by Fischer von Erlach, the Austrian designer of the Karlskirche in Vienna in 1721, gave due attention to buildings in both India and China. It was an approach which was not shared by many of his successors; even Spiro Kostoff's monumental *A History of Architecture*, published in 1985, devoted a mere 5 per cent of its text to non-European works – and then in the context of Roman or Spanish conquest. Even today, the invitation to the world's architecture means passing through a barely opened door.

ARCHITECTURE FOR ALL

Architects abroad

In Britain, architecture did not become synonymous with the work of architects until the sixteenth century. Undoubtedly the masons and other craftsmen working prior to the early English Renaissance, drew not only on their own practical experience, but on the tales of other itinerant craftsmen that we know to have roamed Europe, moving from job to job. Undoubtedly also, the early dilettantes, often clerics – like William of Wykeham, Bishop of Winchester, who was responsible for the form as well as the foundation of New College, Oxford, as well as Winchester College – were able to draw on the experiences of widely travelled and cultured colleagues with similar interests.

The English architect was born of the Renaissance. Indeed, worldwide, the image of the architect as master of the 'mother of the arts', is that of the Renaissance universal man. Certainly early English architects of note like the scientist, mathematician and astronomer Sir Christopher Wren, or the soldier and dramatist Sir John Vanbrugh, fitted the bill well, with their many other accomplishments. But it was an interest in both the past and the present in Europe that brought the English aristocracy to architecture. Then, as now, the traditional, or vernacular, was considered rather homespun and lowly by comparison with what was going on in Europe and Italy in particular, where the rediscovery of the art of the great classical empires of Greece and Rome was causing a sensation.

So what were the problems of learning from history for the would-be English architect of the sixteenth century? Well, first, he had to discover what might be in store for him should he venture south through the dangers of war-torn Europe. In the mid-sixteenth century, there were no books in English on classical architecture. The dilettante may have seen the writings of the Italian Sebastiano Serlio, or he may have seen the distinctly northern renderings of classicism in Antwerp or Brussels.

In the absence of useful published material, the English aristocrat embarked on what has come to be called 'the Grand Tour', in order to see for himself the wonders of classical architecture and the work of the French and Italian Renaissance. Not all these thirsters after knowledge were aristocratic or wealthy, but those that were not had to travel under the patronage and protection of those that were. Much of the study of Roman and Italian Renaissance architecture by that most brilliant of British Renaissance architects, Inigo Jones, was carried out under the patronage of and in company with the Earl of Arundel. In 1614, Jones brought back from Italy a copy of Andrea Palladio's *I Quattro Libri dell' Architettura* (The Four Books of Architecture), first published some forty-four years before. Much of this richly illustrated book is based on the writings of Vitruvius, a Roman architect of the Augustan era, which had first been set in type in 1486. Jones's heavily annotated copy of *I Quattro Libri*, is kept at Worcester College, Oxford. Throughout the seventeenth and eighteenth centuries, drawings of classical architecture, of varying degrees of accuracy, were brought back to England, where they provided the basis for many designs, though often the architect had not seen the original buildings.

During the nineteenth century, the religious and moral fervour of men like Augustus Pugin, architect and author of *The True Principles of Pointed or Christian Architecture*, extended the antiquarian study of architecture to the 'Gothic' of France, whilst John Ruskin, later in the century, made the previously ignored Italian Gothic a respectable subject for study. It must be said, that although the study of old church architecture and Gothic in particular has spawned perhaps more popular 'train-spotting' architectural appreciation than any area of building, the 'Battle of the Styles' as it came to be known, between Classical and Gothic, actually did promote intensive debate concerning the social, cultural and moral issues surrounding architecture and style.

Of course, today's architects receive their introduction to architectural history in the same imperfect way as the rest of us. Until quite recently even the teaching of architectural history in schools of architccture was almost entirely antiquarian in its methods and requirements: students were introduced to past styles through the study of relics and reconstructions. Like their seventeenth- and eighteenth-century aristocratic predecessors, they were urged to go on an architectural grand tour to see for themselves the glories of Greece and Rome. The lessons of past form were taught by the production of measured drawing studies of classical buildings and the employment of classical orders and details or indeed, whole buildings or fronts of buildings, in the students' own compositions. Every school of any age has an attic or basement still full of casts and carvings of capitals and mouldings, and yellowing watercolour renderings of the Baths of Caracalla in Rome, or the Acropolis in Athens.

In our century, the 'Battle of the Styles' has overwhelmingly been concerned with 'modern' versus the rest; and despite a varied and vigorous renewal of interest in history as a generator of form in the past fifteen years or so, as we shall see, this remains the central focus of debate.

At the 1980 'La Biennale di Venezia', the Venice International Exhibition of Architecture, which had the thematic title 'The Presence of the Past', two of the contributors, Heinz Hilmer and Christoph Sattler, included in their catalogue comments the thought that 'the primary interest in Architecture is how it *is*, not how it was developed'. This has been the approach to history for most architects who, over the centuries, have always helped themselves to elements from the works of others. Architectural historians, on the other hand, often seem much more interested in where ideas originated, and how the buildings were developed, than in the product itself.

Historians and architects, we have seen, often have axes to grind. No one could miss the allusion to imperial power in the blunt neo-classicism of Hitler's architects, Sagebiel and Speer in Berlin. Similarly, Soviet Russia's clear avoidance of historic styles, for the culturally unencumbered modernism, in the 1920s and 1930s, is fully understandable.

Yet perhaps the most durable theme in the consideration of history by architects and commentators alike, has been the theme of accuracy and authenticity. In the current era of 'postmodernism', many architects are turning again to the use of classical details and models. It is ironic that one occasionally hears veteran modernists bemoan the lack of understanding of the rules of proportion and composition of young architects. We, they say, revolted against the classic historicism of our teachers, men like Professor Reilly in Liverpool or Professor Richardson in London, yet we were taught the rules. Thus, the argument goes, although the young bloods of the 1930s, '40s and '50s eschewed classicism for modernism, their classical schooling enabled them to compose their work according to timeless rules of proportion (discernible, it should be said, in Reilly's own work on the Peter Jones store in London). What is more, should they now, heaven forbid, wish to construct an Ionic Order with Entablature; given time they could, with scholarship and accuracy.

But as we have said, in our multi-ethnic society, we can no longer ignore the history of those cultures whose architecture Banister Fletcher dismissed as 'The Non-historical Styles'. Recently, the women's architectural cooperative, Matrix, designed a centre for Asian women in Birmingham. 'Eastern' in flavour, the English architects thought they would use elephant motifs in the design of some exterior decoration, because to them it signified the Indian sub-continent. To the clients, the same motif signified the Hindu religion, and would have been entirely inappropriate on a building where the users expressly wanted to avoid religious barriers or conflict.

CHAPTER 4

Changing places

EVERY new building changes the place in which it is set. The siting of the building in relation to the natural or man-made environment will affect the lives of those who move in proximity to it in a variety of ways. There need be nothing mystical in this and indeed the form and location of any new building is likely to reflect the intentions of designer and client within the immediate geographic location and the context of the age. We condition and are conditioned by the form of buildings, as Winston Churchill said: 'We shape buildings and the buildings shape us.'

Making changes

There is an extension of this view in architectural design which is often described as 'determinism', which lays stress on the potential for buildings to dictate the activities of their users. At one extreme the arguments against determinism are plainly daft: it is always easier to walk through a door than a wall and therefore the location of the door does condition behaviour. But it is equally plain that people will only tolerate ill-fitting buildings as long as they have no choice in the matter, and even then, the worse the fit, the more likely there is to be a demonstration of dissatisfaction, however impotent. Our ability to condition buildings rather than being conditioned by them is usually governed by the extent of our social and economic power. Those dominated by the buildings that they have to use are usually similarly dominated or disadvantaged by other aspects of society.

Having said this, it is worth noting that many buildings accommodate a wide variety of differing uses over very long time-scales. Some of these buildings may undergo major conversions, whilst others suffer comparatively minor amendments to their physical form. Old barns have often seen the change from being the factory floor and warehouse of agriculture to being a machinery store, with little physical change. They then are completely transformed to provide a dream home for the late twentieth century. Eighteenth-century terraced houses have often provided homes to an astonishing variety of households with little physical change and continue, almost in their original form, to serve modern needs as offices, studios or consulting rooms.

It can readily be seen that the nature of the spaces between buildings is a major factor in the potential they have to affect the lives of larger numbers of people than the everyday users. The medieval castle with its surveillance and defence role had a measurable range of influence according not only to its size and impregnability but also to communications and terrain. Modern buildings are no less able to modify the safety and choice of people who move past and between them, albeit in a less direct and overtly dominant way. Much of the history of urban form is rooted in the tension between individual freedom and the control exercised by authority. Most significant buildings are the product of the will of one or other power centre in society. Architects should be aware of the way in which their work modifies existing urban environments.

Special places

The gathering together of buildings to serve communities inevitably leads us to consider the relationship between individuals and groups and the buildings that they use. Some towns and cities present the pattern of their development easily to those with eyes to see, whilst others are less forthcoming. The sense of place is often related to the original *raison d'être* for a town. Major river and seaports usually still have enough about them to make their trading origins an essential part of their character. In Liverpool, for example, where the central Albert Docks no longer function at all, the old buildings and basins provide an attractive theme for the waterside leisure centre of the city. A mining village or cotton town may well be identifiable as such for decades or more after the last pit closes or the last thread is spun. The monuments and palaces of the seat of a ruling monarchy will mark it out as a capital of state or empire, long after these have been dissolved.

But most towns and cities of any age are also almost infinitely complex in their history and the responses of their built form to this. This palimpsest of form, this urban morphology, will make a major contribution to the *genius loci*, the special qualities that in combination give any location its unique sense of place.

For many, the consideration of such matters will appear esoteric in the extreme. Even for many architects and urban designers the same will be true. Yet it may be reasonably claimed that it is precisely because so many designers and their patrons have in the past had no conscious regard for the *genius loci* of the places in which they have worked, that everywhere has become increasingly like everywhere else.

Indeed a very practical problem with planned, undistinguished, monotonous environments, is that we often experience difficulty in actually finding our way about in such places. In America, Kevin Lynch was able to establish a notation of city elements that matched people's broad perception of urban places. When an environment offers us enough variety, we can identify districts, edges, paths and nodes in the city. If we return for a moment to the example of Oxford, we can see identifiable *districts* such as North Oxford, Cowley or Headington, on which most people would agree, albeit with varying views of the boundaries. Thames Street, beyond which the ice rink has landed, forms a positive *edge* to the city centre; whilst of the many *paths* that people habitually use in and around the city, the remarkable spatial qualities of the heavily used route from the Plain to Carfax are seldom forgotten by the visitor. And perhaps the most well-known *node* of all in the city is Carfax, the meeting of Cornmarket, Queen Street, High Street and St Aldate's, where visitors naturally congregate to meet and where modern Oxford's traffic is at its worst.

An analysis of these elements by the designer, preferably drawing upon the mental maps of city users, can help in the design of buildings that make appropriate transformations to the locality, and thus the city as a whole. Undoubtedly some concern with place and appropriate form has become an important design issue in recent years in the minds of the planning profession across the world. In Britain anxiety at the progress of speculative housing built with no reference to local character led Essex County Council in the east of England to prepare a 'design guide' for housing. This guide placed great emphasis on the form of Essex 'vernacular' or traditional village architecture. The planning authority was able to persuade developers to spend more time on design, and perhaps a little more money on materials, to produce housing that looks at home in Essex.

Unfortunately the use of this guide as a model by other English planning departments and the introduction of new central government design guidelines for residential roads, which encourage a similar generalized neo-vernacular form to housing layout, have done much to replace one national stereotype with another. In the Department of the Environment's promotional film 'More than Just a Road', an engineer is heard to express ruefully his recurring nightmare of coming across an enclave of the type that the guidance proposes, somewhere in Africa.

Since the coming of the steam railway, regional differences of all sorts have been eroded by the speed of travel. Today, jet travel and telecommunications give to many of us a world experience. This experience, accompanied by the increasing domination of all aspects of the world economy by a very few corporate organizations, means that to preserve the particular specialness of any aspect of life in any identifiably 'special' corner of the world is a very difficult task indeed. Some of the volume housebuilders in Essex build all over Britain, with sister companies throughout the world, and only a real challenge to their place in the market can make them do more than make a token contribution to the remaining specialness of the county.

Yet the people who live in 'neo-vernacular' houses plainly value their associations with the past and place. Market research has demonstrated this in Britain, whilst in the United States there are a growing number of 'condominia' or self-contained residential complexes, where specialness is in the forefront of the developer's marketing strategy. Many of these condominia impose detailed restrictions on the building and maintenance activities of residents, in order to preserve the designed special quality.

The lack of specialness in most of our modern environments has led to greater concern to preserve those parts of our world which have special qualities from the past. The need for the conservation of natural and man-made landscapes and buildings is accepted by most people. But the cost of conservation in cash and opportunity terms is an area for the most heated debate. Few would consider the demolition of the Taj Mahal to make way for a factory a reasonable proposition, or the destruction of Canterbury Cathedral to enable a new motorway to reach the east coast of England. But when we are asked to forgo a hospital to protect a field that hosts a rare orchid or to turn down proposals for an essential airport because a handful of half-timbered cottages are threatened, more people are prepared to argue the case.

Going places

One of the most powerful allies of the conservation movement can be the tourist industry. Tourists visit places for a variety of reasons to enjoy themselves in a variety of ways. The choice of one destination over another will be a complex matter involving concerns of cost, climate, convenience and so on. However, more often than not a major consideration in the choice will be the special characteristics of the place to be visited. A great number of broad appeal tourist destinations, as we have seen, have a significant historic component. In other words the sense of place is reinforced by buildings and their associations of past events which are peculiar to the particular location.

In a world forever changing, the number of genuinely historic places as tourist destinations is inadequate to meet what appears to be an ever-expanding demand. Tourist success in itself can destroy the very qualities on which it is built: we are all aware of the mounting concern about the rapid obliteration of the Mediterranean coastline by hotels and resort complexes. Tourists, ever hungry for the new and unspoilt, bring the problem with them. For many people, Majorca and Corfu are beyond rescue, whilst we look with anxiety at the coastline of Turkey, the newest European mass tourist destination. At the same time, a nervous concern to maintain the historic quality of places that are primarily characterized by their historic environment has led to local control which often results in the development of a great deal of pastiche architecture, keeping in keeping with its context: by order. The commonest limited achievement of this process is the building that vaguely copies historic forms and is constructed in cheaper modern substitutes for traditional materials. Oxford has its fair share of this phenomenon, not least among some of the less distinguished modern college extensions.

This is not an uncontested process. Indeed, for many tourists the authenticity of the place they visit is important. Others feel that we must be true to the spirit of our age, and not ape the forms and styles of the past. Unfortunately, once this position has been adopted, there is usually only room for the stylistic language and forms of the

Modern Movement international style, which by definition is unconcerned with place. In retrospect, many might wish that Coventry's phoenix had risen from the ashes with historical reconstruction like that in Munich, rather than having wholeheartedly embraced the architectural *zeitgeist* ('spirit of the age') of the 1950s and '60s.

Changing people

More than the buildings that they comprise, settlements and cities are the subject of human discourse and reflection. The public domain of cities – the streets and squares and the public buildings – are the places of public exchange and cultural demonstration, suitably laid out and embellished. The private domain – primarily the dwelling – is the refuge where private dealings are played out. Since cities first developed, the definition of the two domains and the interface between them has been a primary area of concern. The forces of good and evil, law and disorder, and the interests of rich and poor have been in contention. Redevelopment of the city is almost invariably to the advantage of the rich and powerful, quite often at the expense of the poor and weak. Commonly redevelopment in the name of reform quiets and quells the mob by reason and dispersal.

Since the explosion of urban growth in Europe as the result of the agricultural and industrial revolutions of the eighteenth and nineteenth centuries, city development has been characterized by a pattern of uncontrolled ad hoc development and the evolution of mechanisms to regularize the form of this growth and bring it within the control of government. The early nineteenth century saw the squalid growth of manufacturing cities like Manchester, so memorably described by Friedrich Engels. The introduction of local by-laws in the mid century, and subsequent national legislation, produced an undeniably healthier environment. At the same time the life of the warrens of lanes, alleys and courts about which we can read in *A Child of the Jago* or Disraeli's *Sybil* was curtailed and in part extinguished. The working classes were brought under easy control in the straight by-law streets of Lancashire cities as well as in Haussmann's redesigned Paris boulevards, or the streets and blocks of the building policeman, Hobrecht, in Berlin.

Amid all the ordering and regularizing, there arose strong

themes of concern with the forms of the rural and urban past. By the end of the first decade of the twentieth century, Richard Norman Shaw, Baillie Scott and others had made certain that English domestic architecture was a model for the rest of Europe. The model was based on a reinterpretation of past forms and styles, and the process was carried on and the emphasis strengthened in the new century by the work of Edwin Lutyens, Barry Parker and Raymond Unwin. In his book *Town Planning in Practice*, first published in 1909, Unwin brought the influence of the Viennese music teacher Camillo Sitte to bear on the English-speaking world.

The works of both Sitte and Unwin remain powerfully influential today. Sitte studied the plan and resultant visual forms of historic Germanic cities in his treatise on *City Planning in its Artistic Form*. In an age beginning to be dominated by orthogonal grid forms, the lessons he taught concerning the artifice of the apparently random planning of medieval cities were vital. More recently the work of Gordon Cullen has demonstrated similar concerns with 'townscape', though in a way regrettably less obviously rooted in an analysis of the precise plan forms of the buildings that generate the views and street pictures.

The economic key to successful city development was recognized by one of the first effective urban design reformers: Ebenezer Howard. In the last decade of the nineteenth century, Howard not only wrote about his ideal 'Garden City' and the collective financial and organizational means by which it was to be achieved, but set about the establishment of the first built example. In 1901, the development of Letchworth Garden City was begun according to the designs of the housing architects Barry Parker and Raymond Unwin.

The architecture of Parker and Unwin, with its references to the rural and urban domestic architecture of pre-industrial England, was as much a reaction to the squalor of nineteenth-century industrial cities as was Howard's conception of the schematic planning form. The latter was the most durable legacy of Howard's ideas, and the diagram shown here is perhaps one of the most reproduced of all works related to modern urban history. The basic concept of geographically zoning the major activities of city life became a feature of international planning which remains dominant today.

The Swiss thinker, artist and architect Le Corbusier was involved early in his career in the activities of the French Garden City Movement, and later translated the zoning concept into his

Modern Movement futurist idiom in the plans for the Ville Radieuse. The mismatch between this concept and the patterns of traditional urban exchange are nowhere seen more clearly than at Edwin Lutyen's New Delhi and Le Corbusier's Chandigarh in India, where poor people toil the vast distances between isolated pavilion buildings that house only the offices of power and privilege.

Following the 'zoning' principle and Le Corbusier's application of it, in the hands of many architects the spaces between buildings became featureless communication channels devoid of any potential for active human contact. The results of this approach are easily seen, albeit on a more human scale, in any European post-war new town, or in many cities in the United States, where the middle-class dependence on the car, the office and the out-of-town shopping centre has recently led to wide-ranging attempts to regenerate the commercially and socially dead downtown areas.

There is a crude utopianism in Garden City thought and the Modern Movement extension of it that was developed and presented by Le Corbusier and his followers at the succession of international congresses (Congrès Internationaux d'Architecture Moderne: CIAM) between 1928 and 1959. The architectural approaches associated with both versions of the similar ideal have produced some fine buildings and interesting urban or suburban places. Yet on balance, the contribution that garden cities and new towns have made has been found fundamentally wanting.

Simplistically zoned cities dissipate the liveliness which comes from the close mix of uses in cities that have slowly evolved over time. Zoning may also deprive the economically and socially disadvantaged of easy access to the full range of benefits of urban life. Women, children and the elderly are often especially at risk: they are less likely to have access to a car and less able to deal with the perils that beset the pedestrian in underpasses and dark alleys. This would be a matter of little more than historical significance were it not for the fact that many countries of the world, now in the process of moving from an essentially agrarian economy to an industrial/commercial one, look to our past development patterns for models for the present and future development of their own cities.

The last manifestations of the garden city ideal in Britain are no more hopeful. Milton Keynes, perhaps the final version of the state-generated new town in England, eschews the neighbourhood concept which dictated the design approach to housing in other post-war new towns. In the design thinking that lay behind the development, great emphasis was placed on the city-wide community of choice that could be provided by rapid transport and modern technology – in this case, the car and cable television. But just like the proposals for private sector new towns which are the current preoccupation of developers and planners, the car-based culture of Milton Keynes is highly dependent for its success on the relative affluence of its residents, and indeed on the continuing flow of limited fossil fuel resources for private consumption.

Despite many efforts in the United States to revitalize the ailing downtown areas of cities – in Portland, or Baltimore, Pittsburgh or Cincinnati, Louisville or Richmond, St Louis or Seattle – suburban housing and out-of-town shopping and recreation have become a similarly dominant form, working against the old urban ideals. At the same time, however, an increasing appreciation of the benefits of trees and plants in urban areas is leading to the greening of our cities. In Melbourne, Australia, for example, a major city street was transformed overnight with turf and trees, shrubs and fountains – for just one day. Whilst in cities across Europe, international garden festivals flourish and we see urban farms springing up for the pleasure and education of city dwellers, from Berlin to Birmingham.

The problems that face architects and others who make physical interventions in our cities now are diverse, varying according to location and the political economy of the culture in which they work. Two themes are common: the first is a gradual but inescapable recognition that we need to take as much *care* as we possibly can to reflect place and culture and to respect the historic resources, both natural and man-made, of the environments within which we work; the second, which is directly related, is that we have to give very special consideration to the appropriate form of development in areas geographically separated from existing settlements.

Seldom yet have we matched in the development of planned new towns, the success of incrementally evolved towns and cities of the past. Whilst we may have to accept that communities take generations to form, as the balance of predominant development moves from work within existing frameworks to work on the existing urban fringes and beyond, we need to be doubly careful that we create places and buildings that can adapt to meet the demands of changing economic and social circumstances. This, at least, is one point of view. There are, of course, many other views. If we accept

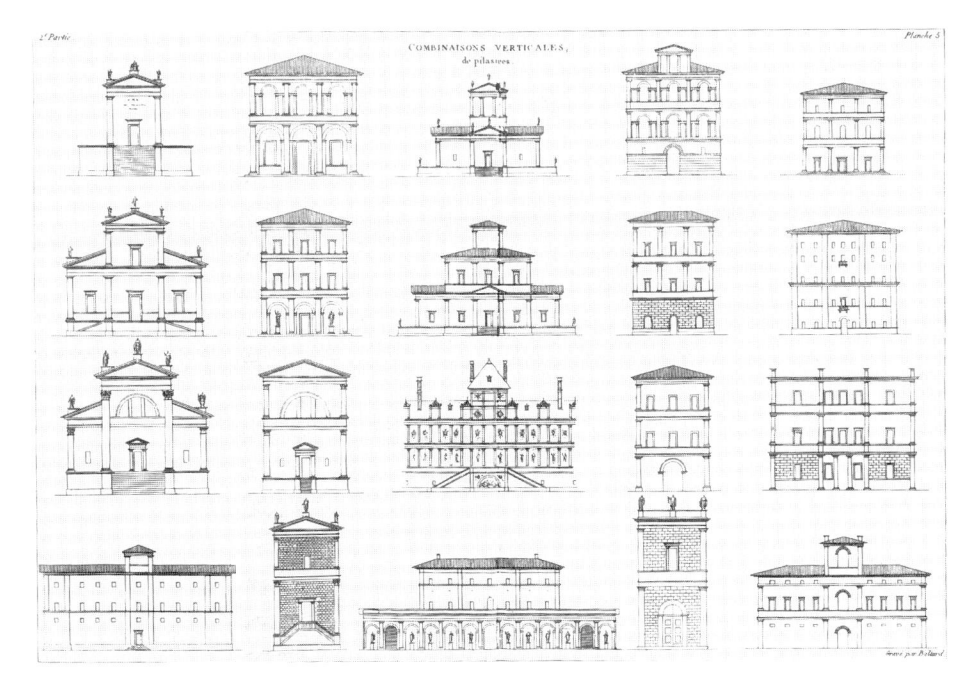

In nineteenth-century France, architecture students were taught the discipline of 'building types' at the Ecole Polytechnique.

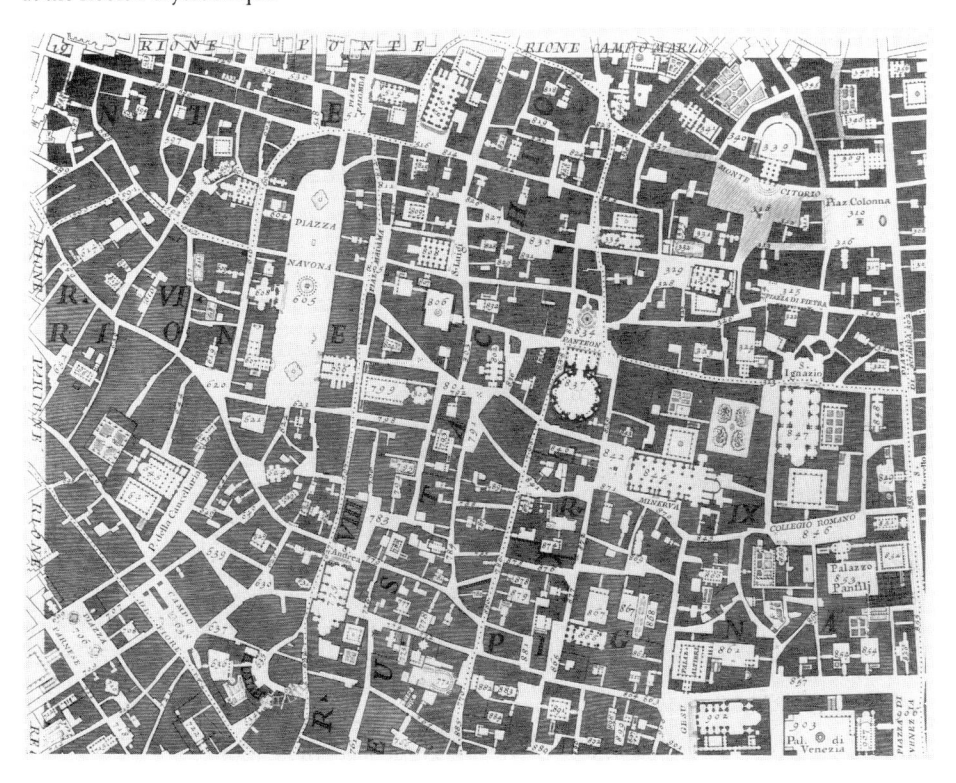

An excerpt from Gianbattista Nolli's marvellous 'New Plan' of Rome (1748), which clearly shows the public spaces of streets, places and, exceptionally, the interiors of public buildings, in contrast with private property.

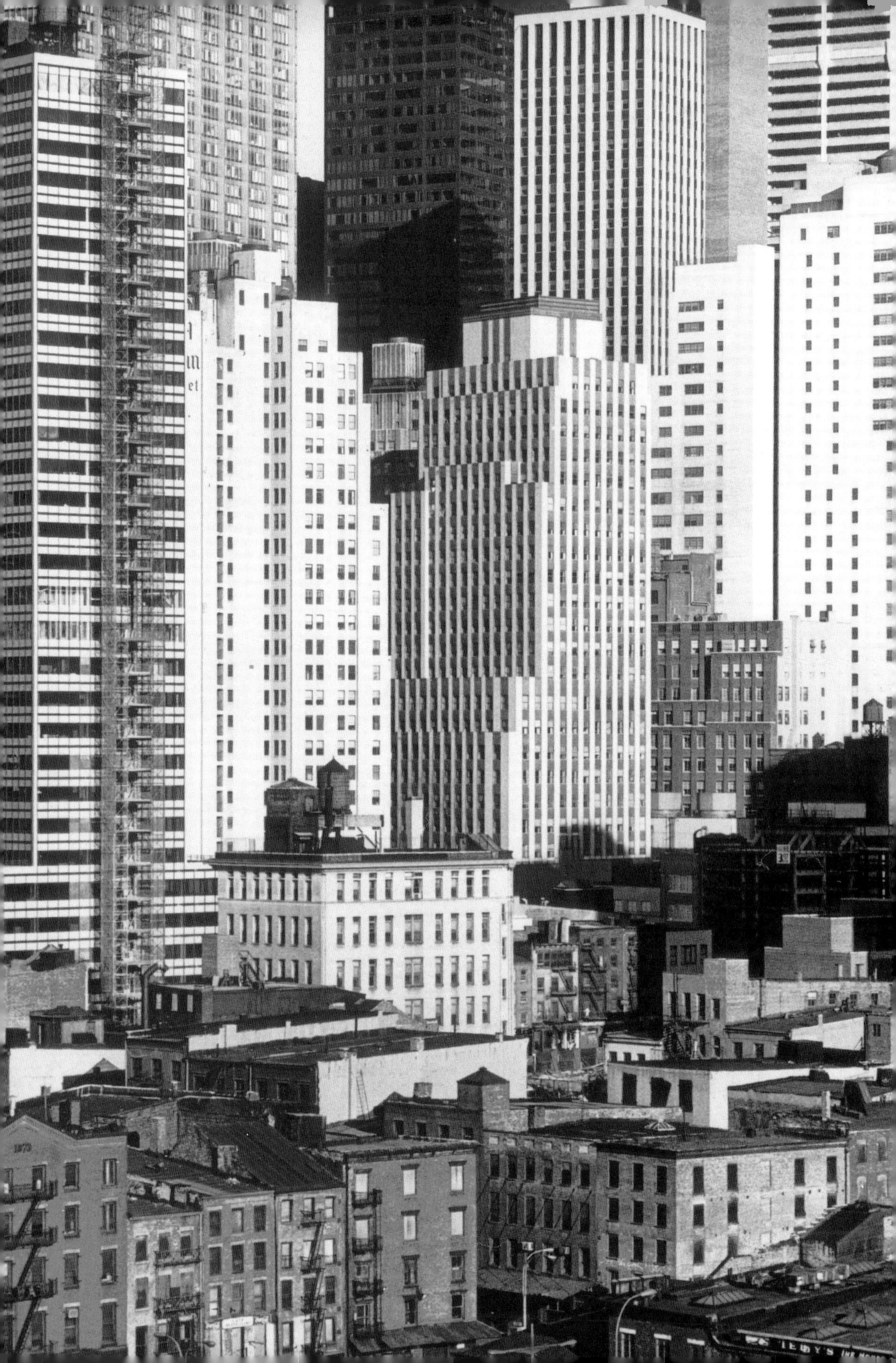

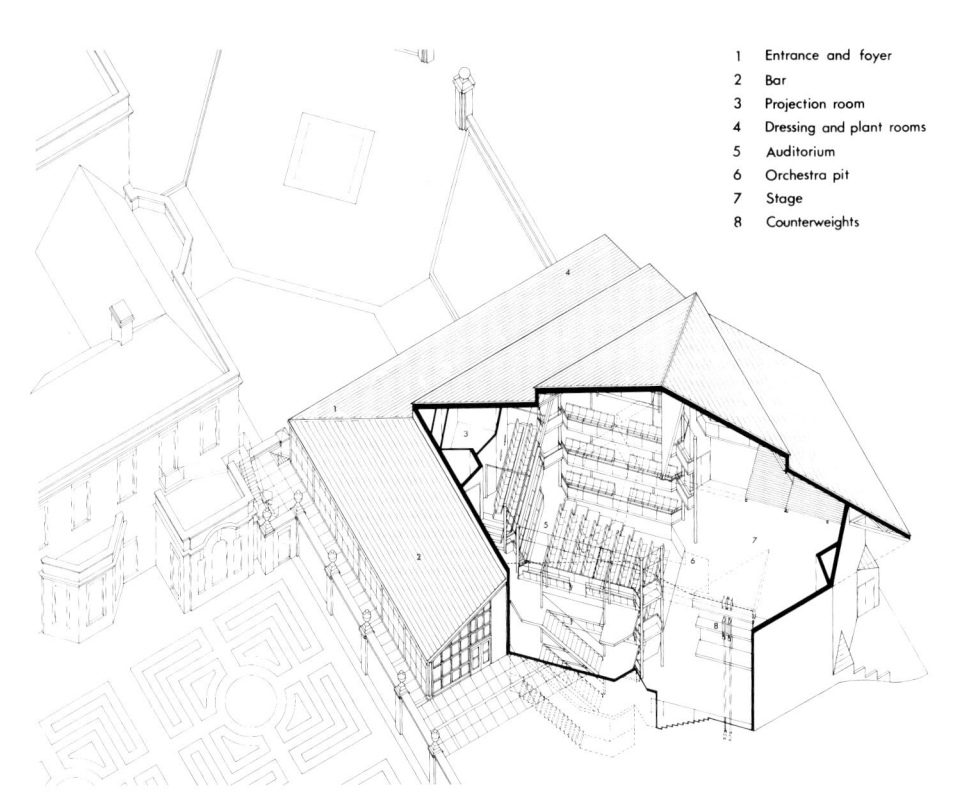

1	Entrance and foyer
2	Bar
3	Projection room
4	Dressing and plant rooms
5	Auditorium
6	Orchestra pit
7	Stage
8	Counterweights

Cutaway axonometric of the Wilde Theatre, Bracknell (1984), courtesy of the architects: Levitt Bernstein. Whilst relatively easy to draw – compared with a perspective – the axonometric may be both striking and clearly informative.

Office or studio? Even though there are architects' offices where computers have totally supplanted drawing boards, it seems unlikely that the mystique of the studio and 'thinking with a pencil' will be lost in the near future. Peridot's multi-disciplinary architecture/urban design office, Oxford.

(*opposite*) Modern skyscrapers, some more than sixty storeys high, rise above the low-rise commercial and apartment buildings of nineteenth-century New York. The skyscraper was made possible by the development of the steel frame, the elevator and the solid bedrock of Manhattan Island. (Photograph: Vic Edelstein, New York.)

The garden façade of the Wurzburg Residenz designed by Balthasar Neumann (1711–16).

Geometric analysis of classical forms. An example from the Liverpool University 'Liverpool Sketch Book' of 1911.

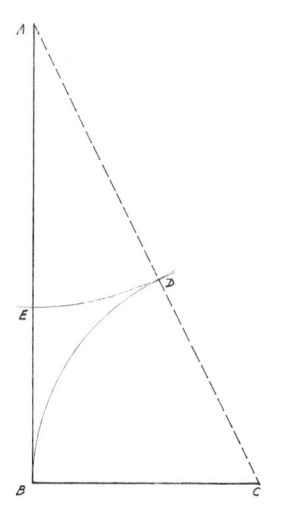

To Divide a line (AB) at the Golden Section: Construct BC at right angle to AB. BC = 1/2 AB. Describe arc CB to intersect AC at D. Describe arc AD to intersect at E. E = ϕ dividing AB at the Golden Section. Thus: EB : AE as AE : AB. (The lesser [EB] is to the greater [AE] as the greater [AE] is to the whole [AB].)

The grand staircase of the Residenz (1737), which brings the visitor alighting from a coach in the covered concourse below to the splendour of the great illusionistic ceiling by the Italian painter Tiepolo. A deliberate movement through vertical space.

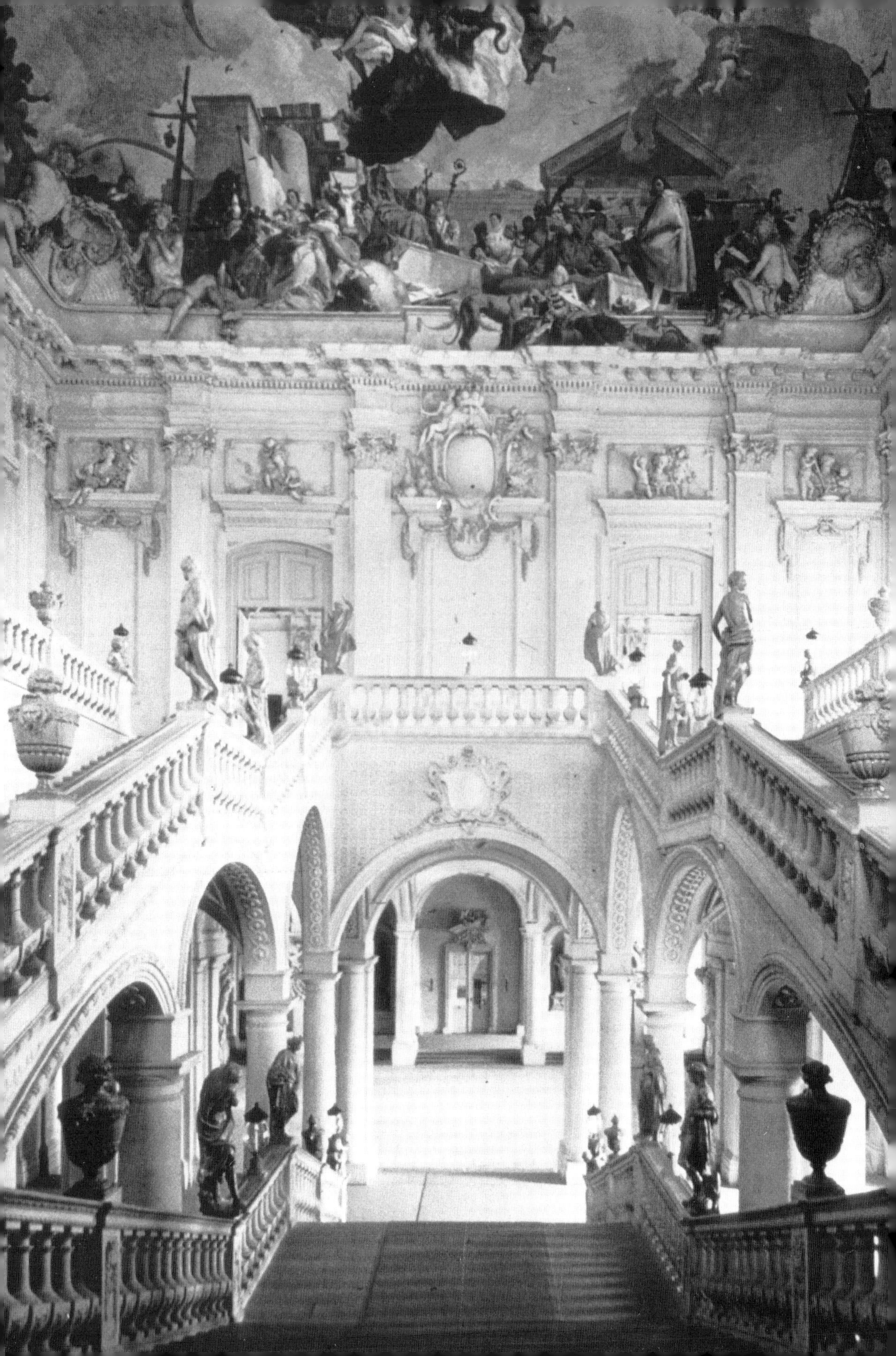

(*above*) Quinlan Terry's Richmond panorama is a tour de force of eclectic historicism, which demonstrates that the skills of traditional construction can still be used to serve commercial demands, but leaving us uneasy about an architecture so untouched by the present or recent past. (Photograph: Charlotte Wood.)

(*left*) Making buildings, in terms of twentieth-century industrial production methods, is still generally a relatively labour-intensive process. (The Architectural Press Ltd.)

Computer aided design and computer generated drawings are an everyday reality of architectural practice. The first illustration (*right*) shows a three-dimensional "computer visualization" of a design for a market cross in an Essex town, by Tony Hall of Anglia College, Chelmsford, whilst the second (*below*) shows a proposed office building, courtesy of SOM, London.

Herman Hertzberger's insurance building at Appeldoorn, Holland (1971). Part of the public circulation space with seating areas for informal meetings. A relaxed and humane modern interior.

the former as one recognizable broad grouping of views, then the equally broad counter position is that which proposes that progress and the future are paramount, and that in spirit as well as utility we should seek to make as much progress in all our endeavours as possible, without undue deference to the models of the past. This is the rational comprehensive approach *par excellence* to problem-solving in the built environment.

Power and places

In the West and in development elsewhere perpetrated by Western influences, this almost certainly means an approach based on the rationale of capital. Even where development is sponsored by Eastern bloc powers the conceptual approach to problem-solving in this rational comprehensive vein is likely to be more doctrinaire than in any way contextual, with regard to place or culture. Effectively, both Eastern and Western powers tend in their imperialism to be more concerned with the reproduction and furtherance of their own models of efficiency than with the apparently regressive cultural and regional concerns of place. After all, both capitalism and socialism now work on the world stage and have a primary preoccupation with economic and social power.

Why should architects worry about any of this? Well, more often than not, the briefing which they receive for all but the smallest commissions comes from branches of multi-national organizations, with ever-decreasing national allegiances. Now at a conceptual level, this may be no bad thing. After all, in recent history, a great deal of suffering has resulted primarily from conflicts between national interests. The worry is that the ever-increasing supra-national interests are far from democratic and are concerned – whether ostensibly capitalist or socialist – with but one objective: the generation of material wealth.

The architect's design agenda, which as a result of most current models of architectural education, will at least in part concern itself with some hazy notions of the 'public good' and a concern with context, may well be significantly out of tune with those of the patron organization. Seldom will open conflict arise in the design process as a result of this. But almost inevitably the architect with her presentation as a muddy booted artist will be powerless and manipulated by the concerns of the funding institution. Organizations that essentially have few preoccupations other than material efficiency will make every concession, and only those concessions, that further their broad objectives. Issues of multi-national identity, success and security of investment, will be paramount.

Changes for living

As the twentieth century draws to a close, the future for the 'old world' of Western Europe is increasingly perceived by many to be that of a tourist destination for visitors from the new worlds of the United States and the countries and continents more recently developed, in Western terms, from Australasia to Africa. Yet even if that is to be the case, we still need to live, to eat, to use libraries, schools, hospitals and shops; and in the best of our cities, the quality of life for many remains unsurpassed in its richness and variety.

Fortunately, too, architects are seldom despondent. In the West, we may see the war-torn, divided city of Berlin as an emblem of urban failure. On both sides of the Wall there remains plenty of squalor and gaping sites left from the war-time devastation. Much of the reconstruction seems to comprise vast highways where the car reigns supreme and the pedestrian has no place. Yet Berlin has been the site of two post-war building exhibitions, separated in time by some thirty years, but both aimed at demonstrating the possible high quality of urban living. These 'exhibitions' were more in the form of Expositions, where the buildings were completed and became part of the city.

The Interbau Exhibition of 1957, mostly set in parkland close to the Tiergarten (although Le Corbusier's 'Unité' flat block is far away to the west of the city), left behind a group of Modern Movement housing by international architects from Le Corbusier and Walter Gropius, to the architect of Brasilia, Oscar Niemeyer, and Finland's Alvar Aalto. The exhibition was a gesture of defiant hope, and regardless of our feelings about high-rise flats or the ill-defined spaces around the buildings, with its mature landscape, it leaves an elegant and tranquil living museum of past ideas of urbanism and housing.

The more recent International Building Exhibition, which was concluded in 1987, took place amid many more published words on the essential vitality of the city as a place to live. Again the architectural cast was international and distinguished, from Germany's own

Professor Ungers to America's Peter Eisenmann and England's Peter Cook and Christine Hawley. But the approach to the built form for city living is quite different. The buildings are low-rise, seldom more than five-storey, and there has been an enormous effort to recreate networks of smaller streets and squares, shared safely between vehicles and pedestrians.

In areas like the multi-ethnic Kreuzberg, with its acres of densely developed nineteenth-century *mietskasernen* (rental barracks), the exhibition has espoused the principles of direct participation of residents in the improvement plans for their housing, often then employing their own building skills and labour in the realization.

The results of both exhibitions are remarkable and have contributed and will continue to contribute to an improvement in the choice and richness of the city as a home. Both exhibitions were the product of efforts by politicians, pressure groups and environmental professionals, but the form of the successes and the failures, were, each in their own period, examples of the best that architects could do to make better places.

PART II

ARCHITECTURE AND ARCHITECTS

CHAPTER 5

Making architects

It is one thing to be interested in architecture: it is something altogether more committing to be an architectural student. If you are studying buildings as a hobby you can do it anywhere, read what you like, see what you want (given time, money and inclination), form your own opinions and leave off when you have had enough. But to be a student, studying architecture in order one day to practise it, you have to be *dedicated*. No one would say it was a soft option. For one thing, there is almost no preparation for architecture at school, so you cannot bring the things you learned with you to the school of architecture studio. In fact, it is very common to hear lecturers and studio staff say 'forget anything you ever learned or heard about architecture, and start again'. Not very good educational policy, for it is better to build up on what a student knows and has experienced already, than to demolish it. Yet there are so many prejudices about architecture, and so little really known about it outside the profession, that it is understandable.

At the present time it takes seven years to 'train' as an architect; only a doctor's training is as long. There are moves afoot to reduce the time; after all, courses are shorter in the United States and some countries in Europe. Within that time though are two years of what is termed 'professional practice', during which the student works in an architect's office, or perhaps in the architectural department of a large local authority, or even overseas with a foreign firm. If at times this means making the tea, it also generally involves a fair measure of responsibility in seeing a 'job' through. One of those years is the seventh and final one, when students have given up jeans and grubby sweaters and have settled for a scrubbed appearance and sober suits. In other words, this is when the reality of having to make a living in an exacting and demanding profession really comes home.

There is an earlier stage of professional experience too: it usually comes between the third and fourth years of the course – between the 'Intermediate' level or, in Britain, Part One of the Examinations of the Royal Institute of British Architects (RIBA), and the Diploma Course or its equivalent that follows, which leads to RIBA Part Two. But that's not the end of it – there is also a Part Three examination in Professional Practice which takes place at the end of the seventh year.

If that seems formidable, well, it is. There is so much to learn about structures and construction, about the physical laws and properties of materials, and how they are correctly assembled. You have to learn about services, the supply and integration of water, drainage and sewage disposal, electric and other sources of power, and the problems of insulation, safety, fire regulations and much else that makes them work or fail. There is heating, lighting and ventilation, central and solar heating systems, natural and artificial light, the circulation and conditioning of air, and building 'refrigeration' to understand. You need to know about the circulation of people, and mechanical systems to aid it, like elevators and escalators. This means the installation of heavy plant, so you need to know how to cope with the 'loads' on the building that they generate. Buildings are constructed these days in a variety of materials, from conventional timber and brick to steel and reinforced concrete, from aluminium and metal sheeting to glass and plastics: they all require special handling and they behave differently in variations of temperature or under stress: all this and much, much more the architectural student needs to know.

These subjects are applicable to the design of individual buildings which, however, will always exist in a context. So, there are Building Regulations to learn and meet, local by-laws and planning regulations to satisfy. Much of a young architect's work may involve conversions of old buildings, so their specific characteristics need to be known. A great many new structures are placed in situations where there are buildings of earlier date to respect, and to which the new ones should relate. This means a knowledge of 'urban design', or of landscaping – which necessitates a knowledge of trees and shrubs that will thrive in towns and suburbs. Because many towns and cities are of great age, and numerous buildings may be several hundred years old, it is valuable for a student to have, for purely practical reasons, a good knowledge of the history of architecture. But he, or she, also needs to study it in order to know how architectural concepts arose, were developed, and applied in the design of buildings.

And what buildings! There is such an enormous variety of buildings that we use in our day-to-day living, from houses and apartments to shops and offices. Multi-storey car parks, department stores, supermarkets and shopping malls are familiar to us all. There are sports stadia and leisure centres, hotels and motels, museums and galleries, churches and mosques, car ports and airports, dining halls and concert halls, farms and factories, which are within the experience of most of us. You can draw up your own list from the buildings which you may use in the course of a week: public libraries, clinics, hospitals – the list will surely impress you. Every architectural student does not have to have practice in designing all of them, but he *does* need to know how to go about it and how to design for the specific requirements of each type.

We have not said anything about *design* as yet – though this is what the particular skill of the architect is supposed to be. Designing involves the bringing together of all these factors, and doing so with quality, even 'beauty' – though that is, or is not, *still* in the eye of the beholder. The architect seeks to create 'spaces' which may enthral or delight, and buildings which give visual pleasure to those 'in the street'. But people respond to buildings subliminally as well as consciously; there is a whole field of study which is concerned with the psychology of architecture, from the use of colour to the sensory perceptions of interiors. If this is a matter of the individual in relation to a building, architecture can also have social effects – or so we all believe when we criticize housing developments. It is sometimes suggested that the social failure of many buildings is related to costs – that too little has been spent on public facilities, day-care for children, the needs of the aged or the disabled, for instance. True: and this lays a further burden on the architect, who also has to work within tightly defined budgets. He cannot cut corners though; the architect is legally liable for any infractions of building codes and standards, even if they are committed by the builder. An architect's liability is a serious problem and necessitates knowing his position in law over many aspects of building construction and performance.

Already that issue of design, the essence of architecture, has become buried in the list of other demands that are made upon the architect. Small wonder that architects often say their work is 'five per cent inspiration, and ninety-five per cent perspiration'! It makes one wonder why anyone takes up architecture as a profession. But thousands do – every year. There are over thirty schools of architecture in Great Britain to meet the demand for places on courses that will lead to qualification and 'Registration' with ARCUK – the Architects' Registration Council of the United Kingdom, the body which permits someone to practise, even when he or she has *not* qualified from a British school.

With all this to understand and design with, and within, it is probably no surprise that a course *does* last seven years all told, of which five are usually spent within a school of architecture. (Not always; it is still possible to learn the craft by working as a junior assistant in an office and to take one's examinations from there.) Hardly surprising either that the schools of architecture are for ever engaged in serious debate, not only as to which, if not all, of these subjects should be taught to students, but also *how* they should be taught. On these issues there is considerable disagreement, for while it is evident that they are all relevant, and important to the architect in practice, there is room for different opinions on which should be a part of a school course and which should be learned through working in an office.

For example, there are some who would argue that the study of Western History in Architecture is essential; others would maintain that only the history of twentieth-century architecture is relevant. Some believe that an architect cannot be psychologist and sociologist as well as designer, while many would argue that an awareness of the issues these disciplines raise is important to the design of mass housing. These are typical problems of syllabus, but there are also numerous questions which directly affect the purchase of specialized equipment. For example, should an architect know how much shadow his building casts at different times of the day and the year – and should a department have a heliodon to demonstrate this? High buildings may be subject to considerable wind loads, and may also create funnels of high velocity winds between them. Should a school have a wind tunnel for testing models of proposed buildings? Or can all this be simulated through computer programs, and, if so, should they be obtained for the use of students, with all the demands on limited resources that computers imply? And so on. Every aspect of architectural education has its protagonists and opponents.

Beaux-Arts and Bauhaus

It is not a new debate, though there was more confidence in a single educational system when the architect's job was rather less complex.

More than 300 years ago, in 1671, the French architect Colbert founded the Academie Royale d'Architecture in Paris. After the French Revolution it became, in 1819, the Ecole des Beaux-Arts which, for a century, dominated architectural education. Students attended lectures by noted architects and also worked in their offices, as well as in the *ateliers* of artists. Exceptional students might be awarded the Grand Prix de Rome, which enabled them to spend a number of years at the French Academy in Rome, housed in the Villa Medici.

Theories of architecture in the Beaux-Arts were classical and formal. Capitals of columns in the classical 'orders' had to be drawn and 'rendered', or coloured in wash, at full size. Designing buildings was to rules of symmetry and axiality, severely applied, while great emphasis was placed on the importance of the plan of the building as the generator of its proportions and harmonious design. Though the influence of the Beaux-Arts waned after the Great War, it still continues in Paris today. Influential in Britain in the nineteenth century, its methods were still applied at the Bartlett School of Architecture at London University in the 1950s, and with the renewed interest in classicism, they are becoming popular again.

A letter from 'an architectural student' to *The Builder* in 1846 proposed 'an Architectural School of design'. The outcome was the Architectural Association, which began as a discussion society and for fifty years hardly realized its intention of forming a school. Eventually it did, and the AA School of Architecture became, and remains, the largest and most influential in Britain. Since 1917 it has been based in three Georgian houses in Bedford Square, London, cramped but effective as a focus for visiting architects and a hothouse for design ideas. Now an independent, fee-paying school for the (mostly foreign) sons and daughters of the well-off, it still prides itself on being in the avant-garde of architectural education.

Other schools were founded in Britain largely as a result of the RIBA's policy on examinations in the 1880s. Several came under the wings of universities or, later, the polytechnics, the latter being more constrained perhaps, by the public purse and by 'validation' procedures. Until 1988 these included approval of polytechnic courses by the Council on National Academic Awards. With a further system of approval by Visiting Boards of the RIBA, a fair measure of comparability of academic standards was achieved without undue pressure on the *ways* in which architecture is taught.

All schools face the problem of how to teach the intake of new students, and how to structure the course. In this, but especially in the organization of the First Year course, the influence of the Bauhaus has been profound. Millions of words have been written about the Bauhaus, which was, for a dozen years, the dynamic centre of design education in Europe. It was founded in 1919, immediately after the Great War, in the cultural centre and birthplace of the New German Republic, Weimar. The Grand Ducal Schools of Fine Arts and Arts and Crafts were combined under the direction of the architect Walter Gropius. The first 'proclamation' of the Bauhaus ('house of building') sought to do away with distinctions between architecture, crafts and fine arts. But most of the teachers were artists: Johannes Itten, Paul Klee, Oscar Schlemmer, and later, Kandinsky and Moholy-Nagy. Itten directed the *Vorkurs*, or Preliminary Course, part experimental, part mystical, in which students explored the nature of materials, colours, textures and forms. Then they went into craft-orientated workshops, to study clay, glass, wood, textiles and so on. A complementary course, the *Formlehre*, was devoted to the study of formal problems – the analysis of nature, descriptive geometry, theories of composition, space and construction. It was exciting, and the output of the Bauhaus was prodigious, its design shaping so much of what we see around us today, popularized through outlets like the Habitat shops.

Yet even at the time the Bauhaus had its critics: it was too art-based, it was not sufficiently concerned with industrial design and methods of production, it was idealistic rather than realistic. After 1923 there were changes in the emphasis of the course, and these were still more marked after 1928, when Gropius left the new premises he had designed for the Bauhaus at Dessau, and Hannes Meyer took over. Under Meyer, a socialist, the course became more pragmatic. The final Director was the architect Mies van der Rohe, who failed to save the Bauhaus from the Nazis, who closed it in 1933. Many teachers went to the United States, Gropius to Harvard, Moholy-Nagy to found the 'New Bauhaus' at the Institute of Design, Chicago, Josef Albers to Black Mountain College. Bauhaus influence was not felt in Britain until the 1950s when 'Basic Design' courses were adopted by schools of art and architecture all over the country. Many run them still to give new students a vocabulary of design forms and skills, confusing in the process, some believe, art and architectural educational objectives. For what is vital to remember is that architects are being educated and trained primarily to make transformations in the man-made environments of the city, the urban fringes and the countryside; transformations that are to serve the intentions of the patron – of whom more later – and the daily interactions of the widest variety of people.

So what skills and educational baggage does the potential architect need before embarking on a course of specialist study? In the past, a great deal of emphasis has been placed on the ability to draw. Indeed, it remains vital for architects to have the capacity to explore and explain their intentions graphically, but many schools of architecture look more particularly at applicants' portfolios for evidence of enthusiasm and the willingness to observe and evaluate through drawing, rather than for examples of fine art work. Meeting the particular requirements of architectural draftsmanship is a skill that can be learnt as part of an architecture course. Despite a fairly healthy scepticism in the profession about the benefits of new technology to the design process, there are already a growing number of architectural practices where the pencil and pen have been almost wholly replaced by the computer terminal, and many more where other techniques lessen significantly the need for fast and accurate draftsmanship. But to be able to make the best of both modern graphic techniques and the hardware and software of new technology the student still needs to develop the skills of visual inquiry and spatial understanding and representation.

Architects use a number of conventional ways of communicating their ideas. Usually these involve drawing. All architects draw, and most of them use the process as an aid to thinking. This means that many sheets of 'layout' paper – and innumerable used envelopes at the breakfast table! – may have notes, rough sketches and diagrams which are the first indications of design concepts. Students soon learn to keep all their notes and sketches, as reminders of their design processes, and a record of alternative ideas they may have had, that may come in useful later.

From the first sketches to the design drawings is a big step, involving accuracy of information and measurement. For this reason most architects use the same drawing conventions, even when simply sketching ideas, and they learn to visualize in proportion so that their conceptual drawings can be converted to design drawings more easily. The most familiar drawing that architects use is the *plan*. This is a kind of map of the proposed building, an accurate scaling of the dimensions of the building on the ground. Generally the plan is taken as a horizontal slice about a metre above ground, so that it can show the position of the windows and doors, as well as the internal walls, kitchen and bathroom fittings and so on. When shown to the clients the plan may even include their furniture in position. Generally an architect also draws a *site plan* which shows how the building relates to the land on which it is situated, and which may show roads and services as well.

Another common convention is the *elevation*, which shows the front of the building, with all the measurements correctly drawn to a scale: $\frac{1}{8}$ of an inch to a foot used to be common; nowadays 1:100 is frequently used and is almost identical. Elevations will be drawn for each side of the building. They will often be coloured, or 'rendered', in a close approximation to the colour of the materials to be used. But a plan is normally rendered in conventional colours such as red for the walls, which can be 'read' consistently in all the drawings. Another important drawing is the *section* which is a vertical slice through the building at a position which will give the most information on the heights of rooms, position of staircases, and such matters as the depth of the foundations or the installation of the plumbing.

Many clients like a *perspective* which gives a visual impression of what the finished building may look like. Obviously there is room for much distortion here, and the client may be disappointed when he sees the actual building going up on site. Perspectives cannot be accurate – you cannot take measurements off them. Architects often prefer to use a *projection* on which a great many dimensions can be measured. An *isometric* projection has the angles of the building set at 30° to the viewer, and the internal corner is drawn at 120°. This gives the illusion of a perspective but all the vertical and horizontal dimensions of the building are accurately scaled. More popular is the *axonometric* projection which has the plan drawn accurately, and set at an angle, 45° and 45° or, perhaps, 60° and 30°. It gives more of a 'bird's eye view' but has most dimensions (except diagonal ones) accurately scaled. There are other forms of projection which are sometimes used, even axonometrics taken from a 'worm's eye view'.

Today, a very large number of these drawings can be done on the computer, the program even making possible the illusion of 'moving through' the buildings in perspective. Drawings can also be fully rendered in colour by computer, and many architects now 'think' with computer aided design (CAD) in the way in which their predecessors used their sketches. Computers can enlarge parts of a drawing for the complicated details of *working drawings* which are the ones that architects make for builders, plumbers, electricians and others who require accurate details for their particular job.

In addition to being expected to know how to draw, potential architects need to be numerate. Modern practice conditions mean that architects are seldom required to carry out detailed calculations for themselves. They are generally supported in the development team by engineers and quantity surveyors and sometimes by other specialists. But not only does the architect need to be able to understand the work of these members of the team in order to be able to obtain the best integration of their work, but he also has a wide range of design tasks related to performance requirements that call for a high degree of numeracy. Many of these performance requirements also call for a degree of scientific understanding: for example, the behaviour of materials under the conditions proposed, or the thermal insulation properties of composite construction. Thus, many applicants to architecture courses have an educational background in physics or chemistry.

Most schools of architecture across the world expect that new students will have some advanced level qualifications in subjects like mathematics, art and physics, and all expect that the student will be able to show evidence that she can express herself clearly in writing and verbally in her native tongue. At a time when architecture is ever more required to be management-orientated, the latter is a vital requirement. Recently more students have been coming to courses with a knowledge of human geography: that is to say, not climatic cycles, geology and world topography, but the interaction of man and landscape, location theory, the nature of city development and the economics of the environment. Few schools of architecture are able at an undergraduate level to take much direct advantage of these benefits, with curricula already bursting with technical, historical, social and psychological course elements, which themselves tend to marginalize the time left for the central activity of design. But the architect has to be an expert in buildings and their architecture, whilst also being worldly-wise about the context of her work – the politics, economics, sociology and industry of the world which employs her to express intentions, requirements and aspirations in three-dimensional form. This requires more than merely experiencing and understanding current and past building types and their styles and detail. The architect needs to be truly 'street-wise' in the same way that business studies students understand the mechanisms of late capitalism in our society. Innocents abroad in architecture from William Morris to the teachers of the Bauhaus have been influential in promoting dreams and art which have ultimately produced wallpaper and cutlery for the masses, but little architecture that successfully satisfies the needs of a broad cross-section of society. Most architecture courses will expect to build on some prior knowledge of the history of culture and its artefacts, at a time when the interdependence of architectural development with social, economic and political themes is made increasingly specific in the work of architectural historians.

The Beaux-Arts system of education relied on a patron–architect relationship rooted in the social economy of the nineteenth century, but certainly provided potential architects with a scope of understanding and a problem-solving capacity that remains attractive; particularly so in one respect: the architect was prepared for the design of all building types, and not led to devote all his energies to making special those things that do not require a dominant measure of specialness.

However, the teachings of modernism in art, so effectively channelled into the mainstream of Western architectural education via the Bauhaus, have led architects from their early formative years to strive for new solutions to the 'new' problems of the twentieth century. This propensity may be fostered by full-time architectural education. The benefits of opening the minds of students to dialectical thinking about the problems of design and production as well as style may also help to reinforce the idea of each building as prototype. The older pupillage system, on the other hand, engendered a perception of architecture that was rooted in continuity. Students learned from the efforts of their master. Apart from competitions, the drawing office was the only crucible for ideas, and was geared only for transforming them into built reality.

If we can characterize the Beaux-Arts tradition in architectural education as an 'incrementalist' approach, particularly as systematized for the Ecole Polytechnique by J.-N.-L. Durand, the Modern Movement Bauhaus tradition may be characterized as essentially 'rationalist'. The advantage of the former approach is that it relates new work very directly to what already serves mankind in a given context. In fact, the Beaux-Arts tradition, or rather the architect products of that tradition, have often been guilty of paying little attention to context, and many colonial cities which not only reproduce the symbols of power of the colonizing nation, but also subject their occupants to accommodation inappropriate to other climates and customs, demonstrate this very clearly. Nevertheless, at its best, the evolutionary characteristics of this system can provide society with change following familiar and tested patterns. The primary disadvantage of the system is that it tends to work against substantial innovation. Prototypical buildings are seldom attempted by those schooled in the use of existing types. One might say that the pattern of technological innovation stemming primarily from engineers in the nineteenth century reflects this. Indeed, the Modern Movement scorn for *façadism*, that is, the application of historically based architectural fronts by architects to modern buildings, follows directly from the stylistic debates of the last century, at a time when architects can be considered to have been desperately seeking to clad new technology in inappropriate forms, or, when architects were concerned to give culturally significant form to the products of new technology.

From school to profession

The general pattern and duration of architectural education is remarkably similar across the Western world. The student comes direct from school, or preferably with an intervening year of work experience, to an undergraduate course in a university, polytechnic or similar institution. After three or four years of successful study, the student is deemed to have acquired basic knowledge and skills in the subject and is awarded a degree or similar qualification. In most cases the student is then advised or required to gain some practical experience in an architect's office, before embarking on a short programme of graduate study, most commonly two years. After the award of a further degree or diploma the student is then required to complete a further period of office training before taking an examination for admission to the profession as a full member. In Britain the title 'architect' is protected by law, and nobody may use this title unless they have been admitted to the Architects Register of the United Kingdom, having completed a course of study and examinations approved by the RIBA. Other countries have different approaches. In West Germany, for example, many students become 'graduate architects' after three years of study, usually in a 'specialist high school' (*fachhochschule*) and as such may call themselves architects. However, in the same country, 'diploma architects', will have completed a similar period of study to their English counterparts in a university or polytechnic, with a longer period of professional practice required before they may set up as independent architects.

In the making of an architect the activity of the design studio is as important as it is in the practice of architecture. During the interwar period and the immediate post-war years when the profession of architecture was consolidated in its present form in Britain, there was a desire within the profession to bring architecture in line with other professions operating in the enlightened capitalist state. Comparisons were made with the law and medicine in terms of education and intellectual and professional development and standing. It was felt that if architects were to realize fully their important role, they must be able to deal on equal terms with the other professions shaping our society. Thus, as the architectural profession sought through the Registration Acts to bring all architectural work of importance to its members, it also sought to upgrade and standardize the level of education required for admittance to the profession. In the 1950s in sharp contrast to the 1920s, a large proportion of architects working on post-war reconstruction had received full-time training in schools of architecture. It was those same architects who defined the pattern of education for the next three decades at the Oxford Conference of the RIBA in 1958. Most architects would now receive a university or polytechnic education in architecture. Part-time study and pupillage was almost entirely phased out.

At the beginning of the 1990s central government was concerned about both the restrictive practices of professions like architecture as well as their long and expensive education/training programmes. We may well see some return to elements of pupillage within the overall education pattern for architects. It may be that we will have to adjust to the idea of *graduate training* for architecture, after a first educational degree in a related subject. This has long been a possible educational pattern for barristers in Britain, and is an accepted route for physicians or architects in the United States. Many in architectural education and practice are horrified at any such prospect, but it could have considerable benefits, and is in fact entirely consistent with the evolution of architectural education over the past hundred years.

In 1874, in his book on contemporary ecclesiastical architecture, J. T. Micklethwaite wrote: 'Any man worth a brass plate and a door to put it on may dub himself an architect, and a very large number of surveyors, auctioneers, house-agents, upholsterers &c. with a sprinkling of bankrupt builders and retired clerks of works, find it in their interest to do so.' The primary purpose of both registration and standardized education has been to facilitate corporate professional identity and thus public confidence and indeed protection. On the whole individuals and groups, whether corporate or community, should be able to establish quite easily what they may expect from an architect under a variety of circumstances; they can also be reasonably assured of a level of competence, established through education and practice. The purpose of architects receiving a university or similar education was two-fold: first, it was recognized that in an ever-more technologically based society architects required more formal scientific education; secondly, the profession realized that if it was to be concerned at the highest levels with environmental change and maintain its position as leader in the construction professions it must be educated to a level similar to other leaders. This meant education to degree level. The more general nature of this part of the educational programme is reflected in the title given to most first degrees, which are commonly awarded in 'architectural studies', with the second part of full-time education being concerned with a more professional approach to 'architecture' and the production of buildings.

When architects were primarily trained in pupillage, that is to say, whilst working in an architect's office, they usually supplemented the task-based practical experience with evening classes in drawing and technical matters. There is no reason why students following appropriate first degree courses now should not similarly combine these with blocks of modules which would help them to develop specifically architectural skills, indeed modular first degree courses would seem an ideal prerequisite to graduate architectural study. In such a course it would be possible for the student to take modules in, say, economics, social geography, business management and art history, as well as modules in graphic communication, materials physics and design. This would effectively build on the common range of advanced level studies that students currently undertake, in a much more rigorous and effective way than is usual in undergraduate architecture courses at present. The disadvantage of the pupillage system in the past was the reliance that it placed on the design approach of the particular office in which the students found themselves. Office practice may vary, but most architects' offices of any size follow equally valid management and production procedures, whereas the design quality will be significantly varied.

To improve the quality of design progressively, it is essential that students are led to evaluate critically a variety of approaches. This is best done at a graduate level when students have a reasonably mature appreciation of the environmental and development contexts of architecture, that is, in the graduate design studio.

Over the past few decades there has been a growing awareness of the potential role for architects as enablers rather than virtuoso form-givers in community architecture in both the West and the developing countries. In part this results from a growing awareness by both central funding agencies and local community groups that an effective way of achieving buildings that will properly serve the requirements of groups without the benefit of substantial capital assets is to provide these groups with adequate capital for development and direct access to professionals and others who can convert this capital into appropriate built form. There are several paradigms for this process. Most can be initially sorted into those that reflect a 'top down' or 'bottom up' approach, but in the final analysis every project reveals highly complex differing patterns of relationships, with different benefits for user groups in every case. Because of the variety of client groups and relationships with architects, the latter are having to learn new skills. These include the development of a wider range of visual communication techniques and inter-personal and group management skills. One British school of architecture has a head whose career has been built on community architecture, and more and more schools now involve community clients in the teaching debate and assessment of student work.

It has long been a complaint in industry that as employees become more successful they are promoted further and further away from the point of production. The same holds for many professions, the path from junior assistant to senior partner leads directly away from the everyday work of the practice towards more and more management and public relations. Commonly this is true of architecture. 'Drawing board fodder' are the lowest of the low amongst qualified personnel in an office; job architects find themselves more in meetings than engaged in design; team leaders are forever engaged in liaison and management and the only drawings ever admitted by the senior partner are framed and have hung on the wall of the office for as long as anyone can remember. That this may be bad for architecture is the subject of heated debate. Certainly the system may lose us some potentially great architects along the way, and may result in more good architects being poorly rewarded for their work. But on the whole people tend to follow the opportunities that suit them and set their own priorities. If we judge architecture as art the case is clear. We normally judge art in terms of the development of the individual artistic œuvre in the contemporary context. Almost all the great artistic architects have in common the steady development of their ideas expressed in their work and reaching maturation late in their careers. These men have remained with pencil in hand till the last and been revered for it. Many, if not most of these figures have also been astute businessmen and effective managers. Yes, they are the exceptions, but their achievements are also exceptional. In terms of education we cannot legislate for this. But what we can and must do is provide effective continuing educational packages for those whose operational needs change, either as a result of their own choice of career path within the profession or as a result of developing technology or changes in performance requirements, the law, or whatever. Both the rapidly developing technology of construction and the ever-changing social and economic contexts within which architects have to work have led the profession to recognize that members must be encouraged to take time out from busy practice to update themselves educationally. In the future, all architects in Britain will be required to take continuing professional development seriously, and indeed prove that they are so doing by undertaking regular educational courses as a requirement of continuing professional recognition.

Schools of architecture are naturally a primary forum for most of the debates that relate to the contemporary theory and practice of architecture. Because there is some measure of agreement that architecture is an art, a craft, a business and a public service, it is not easy to make architects, indeed they mostly make themselves according to their talents and interests. Most practitioners would agree with the Oxford academic Joseph Addison that 'What is great pleases the Imagination' and teaches and inspires, but the principal tensions in architectural education remain the balance between art and practicality and between the relative educational benefits of academia and praxis.

CHAPTER 6

Creating architecture

UNLIKE painting or sculpture, experiencing architecture can very rarely involve a personal dialogue between the creator and the observer; architecture is seldom purely private inspiration, nor is it often privately experienced. The purposes of architecture almost inevitably dictate communication at any one point with groups rather than individuals, viewing and experiencing the product inside or outside, from an almost incalculable variety of locations.

Yet frequently, in the history of architecture, the 'architect', the supreme form-giver has sought to be just that; to devise and execute, to guard and realize his own complete conception of a building. Given, inevitably, is the geographic context, yet contrived by the creator is the transforming relationship with it. Inescapable also, is the socio-economic context, yet the aspirations of the creator, the architect, have often sought to break this limitation, whether in visionary hope or yearning nostalgia. In his book *Architects: The Noted and the Ignored*, Niels Prak has shown how Mies van der Rohe chose to produce 'art' in the form of the apartments on Lake Shore Drive in Chicago, at the expense of the residents' comfort. It has to be said that in this instance there was apparently no shortage of people who were 'so artistic that they wanted to live in that sculpture even with all the unpleasantness – like, for example, frying and freezing in it and being blinded by the sun'.

Perhaps the most famous definition of the essentials of architecture belongs to the Roman architect and writer Vitruvius, who proposed that the creations of the art should display three qualities: *utilitas*, *firmitas* and *venustas*, rendered into English in 1624 by Sir Henry Wotton as: 'commodity, firmness and delight'. It is difficult to better this prescription, though many have cavilled at its imprecision, and we mostly ignore the subdivision of *venustas* by Vitruvius into six further categories. Most successful buildings err in the direction of one of these qualities in excess of the others or even at the expense of them. The strivings of the Gothic cathedral builders for the uplifting ecstasy of religious and spatial delight, sometimes took the constructional 'firmness' of their creations beyond the capacity of the materials and technology of the time: they collapsed. In our own time we see buildings that excite the *cognoscenti*, at the expense of the convenience of the everyday user, and far too many well-constructed edifices that have no shred of delight in their conception or being.

Architecture is unique of the arts in its almost inevitable commitment to the combination of utility and art. In its appreciation by the user and observer it is perhaps closest to sculpture; yet the complexity of architectural creation and experience generally far exceeds that of sculpture. Quite often architecture embodies sculpture as only part of its form. The ordering principles of the art are also commonly compared with musical composition, and indeed architecture has been described as 'frozen music'. But in the composition of music, the recipient is expected to be static and in a more or less anticipated spatial relationship with the performance. In architecture, the artist must cope not only with the succession of spaces, solid and void, vista, light and shade, climate and sound, the assembly of materials and so on, that comprise the building, but also with the movement of both the individual recipient and the relationship of this experience to the movements and experiences of others.

Increasingly since the Renaissance, architects have become obsessed with the manipulation of space, more even than with the form of the defining material of enclosure. It is intriguing that for the majority of Modern Movement architects the interior of any building is organized around the manipulation and interpenetration of defined space, whilst from outside, the buildings are generally intended to be perceived as sculpture in space. In the 'traditional' city, the emphasis tends to be the reverse, with buildings defining the all important spatial quality of the public domain, even if this usually then extends *into* the public buildings.

Few architects can handle all of this with any sureness without reference to precedent. This is true of most art. The creative 'sports' in the evolution of art are connected by periods of incremental change and some would say, stagnation. In fact, much that we value most highly in architecture has been the product of the artist following not merely example, but codified conventions and rules. From the days of early Greece to the present, the nature of 'classical' architecture has been that of composition and improvisation within the discipline of a core of elements and rules which have remained in essence unchanged, except perhaps by the Baroque architects of the late seventeenth century and the 'postmodernists' of today. The master builders of the Gothic churches also worked within absolutely rigid conventions, which united the armies of craftsmen and enabled them to create a coherent artistic whole.

At this level, architecture is a developing language, or series of languages and a symbolic code. In order to 'fully appreciate' architecture that has been thus conceived, we need to learn the language, or otherwise make do with a purely emotive or empathetic response. The Gothic cathedrals maintain their power to uplift and delight virtually all-comers regardless of age, sex or culture, yet few can read the iconographic messages of the fabric with anywhere near the precision with which they were created. Convention and rule concerning the representation of figures and landscape enabled those that understood them to identify the characters and events portrayed. The art historian Emile Male has suggested that a mistake or diversion from the rules, by a craftsman, would have ranked almost as religious heresy. The meanings of the concrete forms and images of the detail could be taught to the illiterate, and combined with the spatial magic of the buildings, would produce an experience that supported the teachings and ritual of the church, as well as fostering the more abstract feelings of spiritual uplift.

The church during the middle ages was of course the most powerful international force in the West. The realization of most architecture is dependent on the support of significant power – social, political and economic. Even the vernacular architecture of peasant cultures is substantially formed by the power of the ruling classes. For example, in parts of the Tyrol, prosperous peasant farmers were prohibited by their lords from building their farmsteads in the abundant local stone, lest they grew proud and independent. We are left with a fine legacy of elaborate timber buildings.

Nowhere is the relationship of architecture and power more amply illustrated than in housing: in Western cultures, the houses of the rich and powerful are ever concerned with demonstrations of individual character, a trend continued, though with less and less emphasis, down the socio-economic scale, until we find in the dwellings of the proletariat every architectural device working to subsume the identity of the individual into some expression of authoritarian or collective power or subjugation. A trivial example may be seen in English council housing, where the identity of those who have exercised their 'right to buy' a home is signalled by the interruption of the one after another 'municipal' blue or green front doors, by hardwood 'Tudor' here, and pre-formed white plastic 'Georgian' there.

The relationship of the architect to art and building is a recurring theme in the critical debate of the product. When discussing the architect or artist, there is ever a tension between those at the one extreme who idealize the craftsman builder as the real architect and those who value only the avant-garde artist, who quite often is almost exclusively concerned with the internal debate of architecture in relation to itself, and the self-referential development of architecture as an art form.

We have seen in the previous chapter that the development of the architectural profession and systems of education has fuelled the debate, which has moved between these extreme positions. In his book on architectural *avant-gardes*, Manfredo Tafuri reminds us that in 1919, Martin Wagner, who was later to become City Architect of Berlin, published the complaint that:

the architectural profession has plunged itself into a blind alley. . . . The architect today learns his profession in school, no longer on the construction site. The architect has lost his link with the artisan's practice; today he is more designer than Baumeister; at his drawing table, he gives way completely to his ideals. This office work trains him unilaterally in aesthetics, unreality, and overspending.

In the 1980s the architect, teacher and writer Christopher Alexander has also returned to this theme, first taken up by William Morris and his followers in nineteenth-century England. Alexander, in both his recent accounts of the building of the Linz Cafe and of housing in Mexicali, stresses the need for architectural creation to be tested, modified and therefore at least part formed through the construction process. The philosopher, Roger Scruton, has suggested that any view of architecture that attempted to separate such intimacy of construction and design would have been 'inimical' to Alberti and other thinkers of the early Renaissance. The cafe at Linz in Austria was commissioned by the organizers of the 1980 'Forum Design' Exposition, and was intended to allow the architect to display his approach to designing and making a building on site. At Mexicali in Mexico, a self-build housing scheme for low income workers, Alexander demonstrated that the architect could assume once more the role of 'master builder'. The Mexicali project is also in intention a 'community architecture' project, with the architect acting as 'enabler', as much as, or perhaps more than as 'form-giver'.

Thankfully, much that has been at the innovative cutting edge of the avant-garde in architecture has only existed on paper, or as art exhibits. From these ideas, those who deal in the real world have taken elements and tempered them with the equally important elements of construction, cost, precedent, user requirements and even fashion. We might consider Sir Joseph Paxton's Crystal Palace or the early unbuilt projects for housing by Peter and Alison Smithson in this light. A critic on a British radio programme suggested that, in a similar way, post-modern luminaries in London had been able to work out their ideas in the design of restaurant interiors, in a fashion that would have been intolerable using whole buildings in the public domain.

There is no doubt that we need the avant-garde in architecture, if only because we need to draw reassurance from some understanding of when and why buildings were built, to support our *Weltanschauung*, our overall view of the world in which we live, with which we relate ourselves to the totality of our environment. Pastiche and copyism in architecture can lead to a sense of meaninglessness in the environment, and debase and undermine the real benefit of truly historically significant buildings and environments.

We may debate the relationship of the creative individual to current trends, in an argument for *zeitgeist*, or architecture that we can recognize as being of its time, because it displays the 'spirit of the age', but usually the buildings that are most influential in the development of styles are prestigious in the context of a society at any one time: from church, country house, railway station ('Stations are the cathedrals of our century' according to an anonymous author in 1875, quoted by Sir Nikolaus Pevsner), factory, office, department store, to, say, art galleries, in our own age. At times we entirely forget that architects are involved in the ordinary buildings of everyday, houses, shops, schools, hospitals, social services buildings, where virtuoso displays seldom occur.

The divide between the creations of the architect and popular culture and appreciation, has been a major theme in architectural history and theory in modern times. In the 1960s when popular art became dominated by advertising across the media, commentators like the late Reyner Banham urged us to learn from the culture and imagery of the consumer society. At the same time, a new international vernacular was being established on the fringes of the Westernized cities of the developing world. From Rio de Janeiro to Delhi, people from the agricultural hinterlands were building whole settlements from the waste of the more privileged. Whether they were living in concrete sewer pipes or shanties constructed of packing cases and tin cans, the universal iconography of the newly urbanized populations centred on the 'coke' bottle and the advertisement hoarding.

In Britain the neo-classicist Quinlan Terry, with his portfolio of fine reproduction eighteenth-century buildings, has little time for the 'punk' post-modernism of many of his contemporaries. Yet in their deliberate dissembly and abuse of classical order, who is to say that these people are not far more in tune with the popular 'spirit of the age'. In the United States, it was a chain of supermarkets – those arch-generators in our time of conspicuous packaging waste – which commissioned James Wines to pioneer a Baroque distortion of accepted ideas of building propriety. In Richmond, Virginia the brickwork is peeling away from the façade of the store, shocking and amusing the public, whilst at Hampden, Connecticut the automobile, the ultimate icon of the 'American Dream', is wrecked and rubbished and finally denied movement by being smothered in asphalt in the car park.

During the past hundred years or so in Europe and America there has been a massive democratization of 'high culture'. Great public collections of books, painting and sculpture have made works of art available to all. At the same time popular cultures have gained respectability. Architects can no longer create buildings to appeal only to the taste of an educated ruling elite, or their professional peers. In our increasingly multi-cultural societies the tasks of design *and* appreciation can become ever more complex. We should take some time to consider some of the more common ordering principles of architectural form.

A sense of proportion

Even when we acknowledge the diversity of incentives that cause people to visit or study buildings, we have to admit that we know very little about what they actually *see* and *experience* in doing so. Often reactions to the architecture are expressed in very vague and generalized terms; the exteriors are 'beautiful', the interiors are 'lovely'. For there is very little architectural appreciation in education, and little enough in the media, so that the vocabulary which many of us have to describe, let alone analyse, architecture is often totally inadequate to the task. Yet a little probing can reveal that most people have responses to buildings which extend beyond these clichés, and which are often extremely instructive of how we all react to them. Façades may be said to be 'in proportion' or 'out of proportion', internal spaces may be described as 'impressive' or 'oppressive', one part of a building may be 'out of scale with the rest'. When 'modern' buildings are discussed opinions may be more forcefully expressed. Frequently, similies and metaphors are used: a modern church is likened to a factory, a hospital to a prison, an arts complex (like the Pompidou Centre) to an oil refinery. Terms of criticism are often more pointed than are those of appreciation, but it is not necessary to labour these reactions any further; what is far more important is to discover what we can learn from them. We have to try to identify the processes that are taking place when people experience architecture, and how these can be translated into more informed appraisal.

Let us consider for a moment the issue of proportion; what is meant when the parts of a building are considered to be 'in proportion' or 'out of proportion' to each other, or to something else. Sometimes the concept of proportion is considered to be the same as 'scale' – that a building is in, or out of scale with its neighbours is a matter of its proportions. But they are not quite the same thing. Proportion refers to a mathematical relationship between two or more elements; it is a property of relative dimensions. Often it can be expressed as a ratio, such as 1:2, which may seem simple, but is one to which we may intuitively respond. Others are more complex, like the 'dynamic rectangles' developed from their diagonals, or square roots, which were the secret of the 'beautiful proportions' of many Georgian buildings.

One proportion has remarkable properties. There are several ways by which a line can be divided at what the monk Luca Pacioli termed in 1509 the *Divina Proportione*. This is a point where the lesser dimension is to the greater, as the greater is to the whole (or the sum of the two). Leonardo da Vinci demonstrated that it was the essence of universal harmony and beauty. The navel divides the male nude in this proportion; the metacarpals of the fingers are in proportion to their adjacent joints; many trees branch to this proportion, like the ash; while any cross-section of ammonites or nautilus shells produces the 'Golden Section'. Small wonder that the

Renaissance architects applied it extensively, Alberti, Bramante and the influential writer Palladio using it as the basis for façades, rooms and details.

For the less mathematically minded, Fibonaci discovered the quasi-series 1,2,3,5,8,13,21 etc., in which each number is the sum of the two preceding. He found that adjacent pairs approximated the Golden Section, 55,89 being exactly in its proportion of 1:1.618. Le Corbusier used the same proportional relationship when he invented the 'Modulor'. He placed two series against each other to produce not only a proportional system but what he believed would be the key to a highly flexible range of coordinated dimensions that would be harmoniously related to each other. But the Golden Section (or Divine Proportion) is not just a matter of geometry or a curious 'series'; its relationship to natural growth suggests that we almost intuitively recognize it and enjoy it. It is to be discovered in Gothic architecture, for instance, where it may not have been used deliberately.

Proportion, then, is a dimensional relationship, often geometric, which may be 'felt' subconsciously or employed deliberately through the application of theoretical principles. A badly proportioned building is an ugly one. This is one of the aspects that distinguish proportion from 'scale', with which it is often confused. We usually know when something is out of scale when we compare it with something else, and particularly when it is compared with a number of elements which we believe *are* in scale. A generation that was brought up with model train sets and doll's houses soon learned when objects were in scale with each other: a toy railway bridge or a set of doll's bedroom furniture which was out of scale was tolerated when we supplemented the world we were creating with fantasy, but when 'looking real' became important discrepancies of scale became disturbing. So much so that 'scale models' became a sales feature in the marketing of toys – and remains so.

We feel uncomfortable when buildings appear out of scale with one another. When St Paul's Cathedral, in spite of its great height and dominant position in the City of London, is threatened by new high-rise and hi-tech commercial developments we have reason to be anxious; the examples of the Vickers building on the Thames Embankment or of Centre Point in Charing Cross Road warn us of the damage done to the visual environment by buildings of inappropriate scale. Standing in the shadows of their unfriendly slabs, with their featureless masses at ground level, we make pleas for a more 'human scale', by which we mean a scale to which ordinary pedestrians can relate and with which they can feel at ease.

Scale is generally considered in comparisons; it is frequently the size of the average person and his or her house which acts as the standard. We put ourselves in the place of the house and feel intimidated by vast structures with which we cannot identify. But there are problems – the populace beyond the walls of Warwick Castle must have been similarly dominated by the fortress, and this no doubt accorded with the intentions of its builders. Or again, Chartres Cathedral must have dwarfed the modest houses as it rose above the small provincial town; was it out of scale with them and the thousands of pilgrims that came to the site? It probably was, with its towers 350 feet and more in height. But it was raised to the glory of God, and its overall scale was not an issue. At close quarters the figures in the Royal Portal brought the soaring edifice within reach of the ordinary peasant.

So scale is relative, its appropriateness depending on the proximity of other masses in the environment, and our measure of ourselves. Games can be played with deviations from normal scale, which awaken that child in us all that delights in the 'Wendy House', or the 'Miniature Railway'. Mannerist artists and architects in the sixteenth century rejoiced in the bizarre, using giant 'orders' and gargantuan figures to excite the palates of their patrons. But tricks of scale can be tiresome; they are most effective when they are unexpected, or when they are intended to make a point. Think of the sombre, haunting atmosphere of L. S. Lowry's paintings of the industrial landscape, which largely stems from his deliberate use of buildings and details out of scale with their surroundings, and with the clog-footed people in his streets.

Important as proportion and scale are, our perception of them is greatly affected by perspective; the harmony of related proportions in an Alberti façade is only fully appreciated when we are directly opposite it. Even then, our viewpoint from ground level subtly distorts the proportions. Similarly, our sense of scale can be greatly affected by our distance from, or closeness to a building; the huge mass of the cathedral at Albi can be intimidating at close quarters, and yet its scale can seem protective at a distance. Perspective is an optical phenomenon which we all experience even if we can only describe it by saying that 'it is the effect of things getting smaller when they are further away'. We all are aware that the horizontal lines of a building such as the window ledges, string courses, cornices or roof ridge, though they are parallel to each other, appear to converge, an illusion that tends to interfere with our perception of proportion and scale.

Medieval artists were not much concerned with perspective, or for that matter, with scale. For them it was far more important to convey the essential, spiritual truth of a 'Madonna and Child Enthroned' than it was to have the supporting figures 'in scale', or the combined throne-building in perspective. We can see that they were aware of the illusion of converging lines but they had not discovered any 'laws' that governed it. This was a matter of great importance to Renaissance artists and architects, and it was the architect Brunelleschi who developed a system of graphic construction that would generate an image on paper or a wall that corresponded with what he could see.

Even so, there were built-in errors and assumptions in his system – that the world is flat, that the horizon is at infinity, and that all points parallel to the plane of the viewer are the same distance from him. The devising of perspective techniques had a considerable effect on Renaissance architecture. Great colonnades, like Bernini's at St Peter's in Rome, were designed to exploit perspective. Some artists and architects enjoyed confusing the visitor with *trompe-l'oeil* (tricks of the eye) wall paintings that created false spaces. To do this it was necessary to understand the perspective of shadows, and 'sciagraphy' (or 'shadow projection') was an important skill to master. So was 'aerial perspective', or the use of receeding tones such as we see when we look across a river on a misty day, to buildings on the other side.

In southern Europe where the air is clearer and the sun shines more brightly, deep shadows are cast, though sometimes their strength is reduced by light reflected from buildings that are in the full blaze of the sun. Architects use both, the strong shadows throwing the sculptural details of the building in relief, while reflected light can be employed to illumine or even colour an interior. Building forms, masses, voids and details are all revealed to us by light; without light we can only grope our way round them, and we cannot appreciate their spaces, proportions, scale, or perspective without it. So the aesthetic of architecture depends greatly on the handling of light, which carries all the colours that we can perceive.

Many modernist architects believed that any colour or decoration detracted from the manipulation of form and space. Whether they were working in Scandinavia or in the sun-baked Middle East, they frequently favoured white buildings. In hot countries these made sense because the white surfaces reflected the sun's rays. There was less climatic reason in northern Europe, but the designers wanted the forms of their buildings to stand like sculpture when the sun *did* come out. Other twentieth-century architects have made a distinction between the colour of natural materials, such as spruce or pine, and applied colour like emulsion and high-gloss paint. The natural colours they accept, even enjoying the accidents of knots in the wood or the textures of stone. But applied colour they regard as 'interior decoration' and hence, not a part of what they considered to be the job of the architect. Some have become uncertain about the psychological effects of colour. Is red 'warm', is blue 'cold', is yellow 'cheerful'? Some theorists believe that the choice of colours in a building can have positive or adverse effects on our well-being. Others argue that certain colours 'advance', or appear to come nearer (such as orange), while others appear to recede. As they became more self-conscious about the psychology of colour many architects have virtually eliminated it from their designs.

It was not always the same in the past, though we have a way of believing that the architecture of history accords with our current ideas. In 1937 Le Corbusier wrote a book entitled *Quand les cathédrales étaient blanches* (When the cathedrals were white). But the cathedrals were by no means always white, not even in the natural colour of the stone that was used in their construction. The immense west façade of Wells Cathedral, for example, was just one of many that were richly decorated and carved with figures, all of them painted with bright garments against coloured backgrounds. It must have been an awesome sight in the twelfth century, even if it might seem vulgar and inappropriate to our taste today.

Our criteria are far from reliable though, and we are quite prepared to admire qualities in the architecture of the past which we would not accept in modern buildings. Think of Venice: the coloured and textured walls of the Palazzo Ducale or the gilded and painted loggia of St Mark's supporting four noble horses, or even the startling colours of the houses on the lagoon island of Burano, are widely appreciated but they do not inspire many modern architects to do likewise. Inside, the interior of St Mark's is dark and the size of the windows is insufficient to illumine the decoration. To some it seems gloomy, to others mysterious. We tend to project our emotions on to what we see.

Rococo architects in eighteenth-century Austria and southern

Built to house the great Exhibition of 1851, Joseph Paxton's immense structure popularly known as 'the Crystal Palace' was totally pre-fabricated, the iron frames erected on site. Gutters and pipes to take rainwater were incorporated in the framing. Originally sited in Hyde Park, it was re-erected at Sydenham, where it was destroyed by fire in 1936. (The Mansell Collection, London.)

An entrance to the 'Metro' in Paris by Hector Guimard (1900). Exuberant 'Art Nouveau' ironwork that still delights. (Roger-Viollet, Paris.)

Otto Wagner's Post Office building, Vienna 1904–12. The bolted steel frame structure extends above the curving glazed roof of the main service hall. The louvred steel columns between the doors take the blown air central heating system.

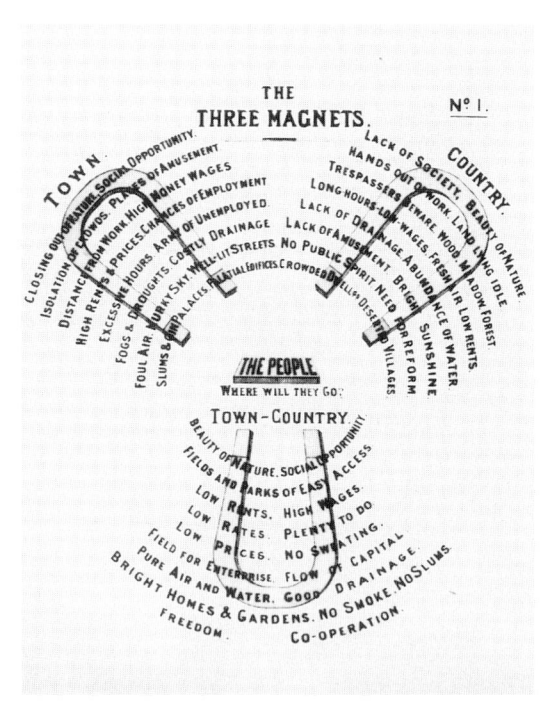

Ebenezer Howard's 'three magnet' diagram, from *Tomorrow a Peaceful Path to Real Reform* (1898), the pioneering book of the English Garden City Movement.

Designed by Peter Behrens, the AEG factory for the manufacture of turbine engines (1909) has an immense frame of hinged I-section members. Despite the echoes of traditional details in the stone façade the building is a forerunner of 'functionalism'.

Massive but basic forms characterized the grain silos of Canada and the American mid-west. This example of anonymous industrial architecture is in Montreal; the proportions compare well with those of the classic portico nearby.

(*above*) The Red House, designed by Philip Webb in 1859, for the socialist designer of fabrics and furniture, William Morris. Drawing upon the clear and uncluttered forms of English vernacular architecture, it heralded a new approach to domestic design. (Photograph: Martin Charles.)

(*left*) Gerrit Rietveld, designer of the Schroeder House in Utrecht (1924) incorporated the principles of De Stijl (literally: 'Style') movement, using broad planes, intersecting members and clear colours.

(*right*) Concrete framing with human detailing: an apartment block on the Rue Franklin in Paris by Auguste Perret (1903), in whose design studios many architects, including Le Corbusier and Walter Gropius, got their start. The panels are enriched with terracotta details which do not impede the broad scale of the building nor its wide glazing. The apartments are contemporary with the Post Office building by Otto Wagner.

(*below*) Rudolf Steiner was not trained as an architect, but the founder of 'Theosophy' designed the Goetheanum II at Dornach, Switzerland in 1921, after the first wooden building was destroyed by fire. He had an intuitive sense of the free form potential of concrete.

Though it is romantic in its concept and siting over a river at Bear Run, Pennsylvania, Frank Lloyd Wright's house, 'Falling Water', designed in 1937 for the Kaufman family, was technically audacious in its use of cantilevered concrete balconies.

Le Corbusier's chapel of Notre Dame du Haut at Ronchamp (1950–6) marked a departure from the formalism of his pre-war designs. The sweeping roof, outdoor pulpit, slit windows of coloured glass and sensitive detailing of the concrete structure, are notable.

The shallow dome of the 'Climatron', a covering for botanical gardens which contains seven micro-climates. Buckminster Fuller, creator of the geodesic dome, designed the structure with its rod and cable space frame. St Louis, USA, 1957.

Rome's Pallazetto dello Sport, 1958, designed by the engineer Luigi Nervi. Though dimensionally vast, the concrete shell roof with its piecrust edge is only a few centimetres thick. The Y-frames are hinged to adjust to expansion.

Completed in 1972 after many vicissitudes, the Sydney Music Hall and Opera House originally designed by the Danish architect Jørn Utzon and engineered by Arup, consists of overlapping shell segments of a sphere, covered in ceramic tiles.

Though the rows of slab blocks associated with post-war urban development created monotonous environments, some American architects combine commercial buildings with dramatic profiles. In Austin, Texas in the 1980s, the blocks stand like chessmen on a gaming board.

Germany used light in a remarkable, plastic way. Admitted through clerestory windows and bull's-eye openings it cast glancing rays into the naves of their churches, reflecting off the elaborate gilding and animated sculptures of pulpits and altarpieces. We can see this in Jacob Prandtauer's great monastery at Melk (1702–36) or the pilgrimage church of Vierzenheilegen by Balthasar Neumann built in 1743. Seen from the outside it is a simple, modest church, with only its bowed façade giving a hint of the splendour within. Vierzenheilegen was designed on an audacious plan of ellipses, and the penetration of an inner ring of columns by light from the windows in the outer wall. The use of light is at once joyous and mystical. Even so, to our eyes much of its beauty is achieved by the contrast of exuberant and lavish Rococo decoration with the clarity of white columns and walls, and the quality of the building appreciated by moving through its elliptical volumes.

There is no doubt that this was intentional on the part of the architect (or rather, *engineer*) Neumann. Earlier, in 1723, he had built a fine 'Residenz' for Johann Philip Franz von Schönborn, the Prince–Bishop of Wurzburg. Its plan was symmetrical, and the prince's visitors arrived by coach at the centre of a noble *cour d'honneur*. Leaving the coach in a covered hall they would ascend a great staircase which became more grand as they rose to a huge landing spanned by the largest ceiling of the day, painted with breathtaking *trompe-l'oeil* illusionism by the Italian master Tiepolo. Balthasar Neumann's Wurzburg Residenz was designed to provide an exhilarating experience vertically through space by the use of the staircase and the 'apotheosis' painted above.

Experientially, such architecture combines movement through spaces with proportional relationships, contrasts of scale, perspective illusion, with mass, tone and colour revealed through light. All these, handled with mastery, depend largely on visual perception for their effect. Nevertheless, climbing the stairs at Wurzburg is a kinaesthetic experience, which can only be fully realized through one's own movement. It's a tactile experience too, as your hands pass over marble mouldings or feel the forms of straining caryatids. Acoustically, the opening up of the landing space is audible even today, while the exchange of smells of horses and hide coach seats in the concourse below for the perfumed and carpeted halls, or the chill of the exterior for the warmth from the great ceramic stoves in the Prince–Bishop's apartments would have been appreciated by the visitors of another age.

Discussing the aesthetics of architecture in this way has the effect of dismembering it. Part of the creative process of architectural design is deliberate and intellectually calculated; part of it is intuitive and 'felt'. And that too, is how architecture should be enjoyed. We need to be aware of the theories and the thought that have shaped the design of a building, and to understand something of the technology and skills that have gone into the making of it. Ultimately, the appreciation of architecture lies just as much in sensory experience. It is true that architecture seldom moves people to tears as music may; but it may inspire by its presence, by enveloping us, and by arousing within us that combination of aesthetic inspiration and intellectual stimulus that we call 'wonder'. Such as we may experience when we first set foot in the house in Lincoln's Inn Fields that Sir John Soane designed for himself in the early nineteenth century.

CHAPTER 7

Practising architecture

FEW people employ an architect even once in a lifetime. Few architects design individual houses for private clients. Unlike doctors, teachers, solicitors or clerics, architects do not meet a general cross-section of the population as clients during their day-to-day practice. This remove from the everyday activities of ordinary mortals lends architects an image which can be flattering and glamorous, with the disadvantage that few people have a clear idea of what precisely architects do.

In marketing literature, houses are sometimes described as being 'architect designed', whilst most people assume that larger buildings are the product of the architect's drawing board, often to the chagrin of the other members of the building design and production team. A common image of the architect is of a man – seldom are women thought of as architects – working in a small studio, with perhaps an assistant and a secretary. Practice is limited to discussions with clients, drawing and visits to buildings in progress to ponder their qualities and ensure that operatives are following the drawings. In novels and films architects offer a compulsive combination of the artist and the master of technology.

So who does employ an architect and why and how do they commonly operate? Naturally the answer to these questions is far from straightforward, both because the range of work in which architects are involved is very wide, and the nature of their modes of practice is also very varied. Like the term 'doctor' or 'physician', the title 'architect' in some countries is protected, and is a general term which belies a considerable range of specialism. Many have bemoaned the separation of the title surveyor from that of architect: Sir Christopher Wren, one of Britain's most accomplished architects, was Surveyor to the King's Works, as were many famous predecessors and successors to the post of what otherwise might be termed 'architect laureate'. And in England still there remains a flourishing profession of surveying with many specialist branches from building and land surveying to quantity and mineral surveying. Many large concerns will still turn to the surveyor for the maintenance or extension of existing buildings as well as for the design and construction supervision of small projects and especially of new buildings which are part of an existing complex.

In fact, when we look at the history of architectural practice in the United Kingdom over the last half century, we find in the first instance that despite the legal and Parliamentary protection of the title 'architect', many other groups are involved in the design and construction supervision of buildings both *instead* of architects and alongside them as part of a multi-disciplinary team.

Whilst some architects may dislike both tendencies, they are natural enough given the often ill-defined and generally varied expectations of service anticipated from architects, and, it must be said, delivered by them. Professional status and the examination passes required for admission to the profession are intended to secure a general level of competence in design, construction knowledge and professional practice conduct, which they undoubtedly achieve. But architects may be the purveyors of art, and this last, and to many practitioners and clients alike most important, commodity is the one that causes most, if not all the problems. For art is beyond the assessment of competence in so muddy-booted a profession, and style and its development often beyond the comprehension and control of the most expert client. Indeed in the nineteenth century most renowned architects were willing and able to turn their hand to any style to please a client in a manner distinctly absent from the conduct of practice by 'known designers' today. Now, you may have what style you will, but you must first choose the purveyor and accept his latest development of the *oeuvre*. Ultimately, most observers have to accept that buildings will be valued as they present themselves and are appreciated by a wide variety of users and observers, most of whom will have no idea of the nature of the creators nor the context or problems of creation.

In the 1950s in Britain many of the most pretentious architects – pretentious in the true sense of having a mission and a message – practised in the public sector. The London County Council architects' offices had 2,500 employees of whom 500 were either fully or partially qualified architects. Like the city architects of Vienna or Berlin in the inter-war period they made architecture of ordinary buildings – social housing, schools, hospitals, health centres. By the 1970s, when much of this public architecture had suffered from failures in production and function, and the public sector was no longer a vital forcing-house of style, architects with pretention viewed both the ambience and the products of the public sector with distaste. In his book Niels Prak has shown that the tension and gulf between the artist architects and the non-artist architects has been a major factor in the development of form in the second half of the twentieth century.

In most countries the conduct of architects in winning commissions has been tightly controlled. In some countries architects may openly advertise where they may do so, the content and claims of the advertisement are strictly limited. Professional institutions ensure that one practitioner does not steal the work of another, or indeed take up a commission simply because a client is dissatisfied with another architect, without agreement from all parties or the adjudication of the institution.

Architectural practices commonly get started on the basis of winning a public competition or the placing of a commission through some personal contact – not a few architects have started with a commission for a house from parents, in-laws or friends. Public competitions play a varied role in the work load of architects according to their country of location. In Britain, despite the efforts of government, competitions play a relatively small part in the day-to-day work of most architects. In this country they tend to be restricted to very large projects of regional or national importance, with the concomitant long odds of winning as they are usually entered by hundreds of architects and students – often from all over the world. Unlike in West Germany, entry to competitions is seldom restricted by the geographical location of architects' practices. In Germany, competitions are very much more a part of general practice. Quite small local public projects are put out to competition, with entry restricted to architects practising in the region or even the immediate locality. There are also larger competitions of regional or national standing. Whilst the British have a very bad record of rarely awarding the commission to the competition winner, this is almost inevitably the outcome of German competitions, and thus the effort and cost of competition entry is offset not only by the chance of winning a prize, but also the chance of gaining the commission with its longer term profit and advertisement potential.

The latter is a vital part of the architect's practice promotion. Whilst the cynic may argue that clients seldom consider the quality of the product, a portfolio of completed buildings, preferably with satisfied clients, is one of the strongest attractions that an architect can offer to a potential client.

Programme in practice

Leaving aside competitions for a moment, let us consider the likely pattern of events from the point where an architect is asked to make a proposal for a new building, to the point where it is completed and handed over to the client. In giving this account, it will be useful to try to dispel some popular misconceptions and also to draw out the likely differences dependent upon the type of client, site and building.

Our first consideration on an approach from a potential client is the brief: that is, what is it that the client wants us to do for him or her? The diversity of both the presentation of briefing material by clients and what may be called the briefing process – the dialogue between client and architect to arrive at a clear architectural brief – is staggering.

Most general and popular accounts of this process rely on personalized simplifications that are far removed from the everyday experience of practice. First, who is the client? We know of Frank Lloyd Wright's discussions with Mrs Kaufmann or Le Corbusier's specially designed bath for Madame Savoye. But most architects operating on any scale prepare most of their commissions for larger public or private 'clients' who are neither individuals nor often represented by individuals. Meeting the client may mean making a presentation and answering questions at a board meeting; the briefing process for a hospital may involve a whole programme of meetings with special 'client' committees of doctors, nurses, administrators and surveyors. In these situations the architect's ability to record decisions, explore and present options and identify both the hierarchy of problems and power is paramount.

When we look at 'the brief' itself, similar difficulties arise. Not only must the architect temper every client's ambitions with the limits of possibility according to cost, but unless the client employs a professional as 'expert client', there will often be considerable discrepancy between the client view of problem and solution and the architect's view of the same.

In the 1960s there was considerable interest and research into architects' attitude and approach and mechanisms for problem-solving. With an arrogance born in the greater part from Modern Movement teachings, much of this work was interpreted by architects as showing that they had a sure ability for perceiving other people's problems, better than they themselves. The dialectically supple architect, unfettered by history or custom, could gather the facts and reorder and rotate them in his mind and on paper, until both the real problem and, ergo, the appropriate solution, became apparent. Thus the solution to a pressing housing shortage was high density 'streets in the air', and W. R. Box could offer the Central Electricity Generating Board not a building at all, but the right hole in the ground, in which to test their power pylons.

In many areas of building, architects have considerable expertise, derived from repetitive involvement in the processes of briefing, design and production of particular building types, which clients, expert or not, lack. The design agenda of the architect is thus already highly developed when he comes to the next task in hand. His responses during the briefing process will be illustrated by powerful references to recent experience in a focused way that may be beyond the resources of the client. In such a situation it is possible for the architect's experience usefully to supplement and guide the briefing process; it is also possible for it to subvert the concerns of the process and move away from the legitimate concerns of the particular client to those of the architect.

A major problem in this is that the architect's experience is usually at its least in terms of systematic user feedback. Seldom do architects have access to detailed user response to their design solutions. It may well be that clients have little reliable feedback from other buildings, but at least their primary concern is the building in use, while that of the architect is often the building in production. For many architects influenced by the Modern Movement every building must be a new solution, or must at least incorporate many new ideas and re-interpretations of problem and solution as possible. This may lead to prototypical solutions which can only be tested by use, at the cost of both client and user.

The likely difference between client, or as some would prefer, patron, and user, must also be considered. If we return to the example of the private house commission, then here the wishes and identity of client and user may well be one, though if the money for the realization of the project is to be borrowed, the financial institution may well interfere in the process. In Britain, the paucity of flat-roofed housing probably has as much to do with the caution of building societies as with the conservatism of clients.

Clients/patrons may well have the interests of users at heart, but like the architects, may have little or very selective information concerning the needs and desires of user groups and individuals. In housing this has led to international concern in the 1980s with user involvement in design. In Holland where this concern was first taken up in the 1960s, the architect Hermann Hertzberger was given the opportunity to extend user participation to the design of the office workplace, and his Centraal Beheer offices remain a remarkable testimony to this approach, albeit for an unusually enlightened and wealthy client organization.

In the changing economies of the developed and developing world, architects are working increasingly with community groups. From the flood plains of the Nile to the north of Liverpool, projects commonly combine domestic shelter with community employment initiatives. 'Community architecture' became a catch-phrase – in Britain with royal support. Even though many projects develop in politically charged situations, most governments perceive the benefits of community self-help. Yet to participate architects have to extend their range of communication skills. In addition the price that they have to pay for close liaison with the client/user is endless meetings and debate, and some would say the subjugation of architectural ambitions to the will of the group. The rewards include the pleasure of working with people for whom the architectural experience and its products are liberation.

So far we have looked at some of the complications and complexities arising from the nature of the client/patron and the brief. In doing so, we have been drawn to a passing examination of the different agendas and conflicts of interest between client, user and architect. Now what about the land upon which the project is to be realized? Many young architects arrive in practice with the firm belief that projects come to the office with a site plan outlined in red and a piece of real estate to visit and carefully consider prior to the development of both brief and sketch design. Multi-disciplinary teaching in schools of architecture lays great importance on site analysis and investigation as a prerequisite to intelligent, professional design activity. Yet in practice, sites are seldom any more clearly given than briefs. Even where a site plan is offered, more often than not, actual boundaries remain clouded in mystery until well into the production process.

So what conspires to make even the clear allocation of a site for a project unlikely? Usually at the root of the problem is economics. Land is a valuable commodity anywhere, but where building development is likely to be viable, its value soars. In the south-east of England the ratio of the value of agricultural land to development land can exceed 1:1000. Many young architects have little appreciation of the fact that land value is directly related to the 'hope value' in terms of likely future development use. The relative demand for particular building types can mean major variation in terms of value for land to be used, say, for small workshops, compared with that to be used for the development of luxury housing. The opportunities for land-banking in highly developed urban areas diminish rapidly with the intense competition for development.

So we can see that the economics of holding sites for development is one reason why a client may start with the need for a building before being able to offer a clear site. A second reason why the site may not be clearly given is that often a client simply has little idea of the site requirements of a likely appropriate built solution to his accommodation problem.

Contrariwise, sites often beget buildings. Planning and building development control is usually rooted in a concern for health and the environmental well-being of society. This generally means that part of the control system becomes distilled into a rule of thumb for areas or volumes of buildings of a given type permitted on sites in a given area. Housing is commonly controlled in terms of 'density', that is, the number of people accommodated in a given area, although it may also be controlled by the ratio of the built to the unbuilt area of a site. Normally the density of development permitted in urban areas will be higher than in fringe or rural areas – a reflection of both pressure for development and consequent values, and the concern of planners to reflect the quality and character of existing man-made environments.

Now a housing developer who sees a site in an area with a buoyant market coming up for sale may commonly ask an architect to assess just how much housing of what types can be developed on this site. Thus both consideration of site and brief are open ended and very much in the hands of the architect, although of course the proposed outcome is entirely subject to the approval of the client. It has to be said, however, that it is also far from unknown for architects to have located sites and prepared appropriate projects before going in search of a client!

Perhaps the best advice any architect can follow when considering a site is to look beyond the boundaries. In most cases site boundaries, when given, reflect only ownership boundaries. The client is striking a deal with an owner for a piece of land, and thus this piece of land becomes the site for the project. Now whilst the assembly of sites by purchase from a number of owners may be a nerve-wracking, complex and costly business, it can in the end produce a site tailored to the purpose of the development rather than forcing development to fit on what may be a highly inappropriate site. Further, in many cases, new development can enhance the character and hence the value of adjacent land. The speculative developer will always have an eye on sites nearby to his current or projected operation; architects benefit by doing the same.

Design and management

Having established the nature of the site and arrived at the clearest possible brief, the design solution becomes the paramount concern. Just as the consideration of site and brief can be an interactive process, so also will the process of design develop and change the brief and alter and adjust the perceptions of the site. There is no doubt that the concretization of design ideas in sketch and model form can have a powerful influence on thinking about the overall potential as well as the detail of how a place might be transformed for the purposes in mind.

Exactly how design takes place in an architect's office is both difficult to generalize about and, in terms of the thought processes involved, way beyond the scope of this book. Much research has been carried out into the design process, which is seen to be a highly complex and synthetic skill. Certainly for most of the twentieth century it has been regarded as the paramount skill of the architect. The project teaching methods that have been habitually employed by architecture schools are fast becoming an educational model for many other disciplines in secondary and higher education. Although the design process remains mysterious and personal, we may perceive something of it in an architect's use of precedent and types. By comparing such precedents with his finished project we can appreciate the element of creativity in his design.

The management of design within offices certainly varies considerably. In offices led by strong artist architects, or would be artist architects, there is often a very centralized control of design at all levels. This form of office organization has a long history. In nineteenth-century drawing offices, the principal sat at the end of a large room with his assistants facing him; assistants would be summoned to be instructed in the development of the master's sketches and be regularly required to submit their working-up for comment, amendment and approval. At the same time both then and now, architects with a major concern for their own perception of design quality would employ assistants whose work they reckoned had sympathetic useful qualities. Thus at times more senior assistants might be given their head to develop a design in the name of the master.

In larger offices, the management of all work, including the design process, is always an issue. In most offices, proximity to design brings kudos even where the exercising of other skills brings more tangible rewards and status. Artist architects are generally wary of the growth in size of their offices, primarily because of the problem of keeping control of design. Whilst in larger offices staff are commonly grouped in teams with team leaders often responsible to a particular partner in the practice, it is not uncommon for offices to impose a specific design control mechanism. In some offices this may take the uncomfortable form of a peripatetic design team, which advises, amends or even wholly takes over the principal design task on projects, leaving to the team the preparation of production information and project administration.

However design is managed in a larger architects' office, there tends inevitably to be a considerable degree of specialization in many. This may take the form of specialist teams concerned with particular building types – at least one well-known London practice divides its energies between theatre and housing design – or it may be that particular individuals perform functions that are only part of the design/production process – sketch design, construction detailing, or contract management.

Earlier, we set ourselves the task of commenting on the activities of architects from the inception to the completion of a project. Whilst we have spent most time in discussing clients, briefing, the site and design, in practice these make up only a fraction of the architectural experience.

By far the greatest proportion of the time of most salaried architects is spent in the preparation of production information for contractors, gaining statutory approvals for the proposals and the monitoring of the construction process on site. The former task involves reference to a wide range of guidance, regulatory and product information, as well as considerable liaison with other consultants. The latter usually puts most demand on the architect's skills as a negotiator and mediator, and sadly is the commonest route to litigation in architectural practice. This is hardly surprising since the quality of the consultants' ability to design in detail and the contractors' ability to construct are both put to the test in what is almost invariably in part a prototypical situation.

Generally, the architect helps the client to select the main contractor. Since most construction jobs of any consequence are the work of not just one contractor, but a whole range of separate specialist companies, the opportunity for dispute is endless. The precise role of the architect in this process varies across the globe. Constantly redefined in the courts, it is essentially that of observer and expert paymaster, ensuring that the client gets the product he has ordered, and the contractor the right payment for the work.

In England, architects have long divested themselves in all but the smallest projects of the responsibility of measuring building quantities and costs. The result has been the rapid growth during this century of the new 'profession' of quantity surveyor. Elsewhere in the world, even where quantities and costs are measured in architects' offices, the task has generally been devolved on to the shoulders of some specialist assistant. Increasingly in England, where offices are large enough, they retain their own in-house quantity surveyors.

At the completion of construction it is the architect who releases the contractor and arranges the handover of the building to the client. Depending on where we are on the globe, the architect then remains responsible for the fitness of the building for its purpose for a limited defined period or eternity. Certainly, lawyers and insurers seem to profit rather more than architects or clients from liability insurance. One Arizona firm of architect/developers employs no less than eighteen attorneys (lawyers) on its staff, who deal with all legal issues from the drawing up of contracts, to land rights and disputes and the complex liabilities of the firm in relation to builders and clients. This is a topic to which architects everywhere must pay serious attention, however reluctantly.

Whilst the stereotype of architectural practice can be seen across the world, since the 1950s there has been considerable diversification in modes of practice. Whereas previously the major differences between practices were probably related to whether they were 'commercial' or 'non-commercial', or to the building types in which they specialized, now we see considerable significant variation in the way that both major practices and one-man concerns operate.

Three distinct areas first come to mind: proximity to the industry; inter-disciplinary working arrangements; modern office technology. The first and second are ideologically related, though, many would argue, quite different, in their implications for the designer; the last is having a revolutionary effect on large and small practices alike.

In the West, the 1930s were a period of unprecedented growth and organization in the building industry, which for the first time could rely on a steady flow of public service contracts as well as commercial work. This trend was sustained by the enormous reconstruction tasks at the end of the Second World War. They led in the 1950s and 1960s to the establishment of new relationships in the industry, and the growth of what came to be known as 'package deals', made and executed by 'package dealers', who were usually ex-building construction companies turned into developer/construction companies employing their own consultants, including architects. The benefit to the client in the package was the simplicity of the contract agreement with one organization and the promise that the many problems that often beset construction as a result of minor disputes between the many parties involved in the construction process would be avoided. Essentially, the package deal offers a known product at a known cost delivered at a known time. Inherent in this promise, of course, are some of the drawbacks: likely stereotyping of building solution and inflexibility to particular client requirements.

Whilst some architects were becoming very excited about the prospect of actually working for the contractor, rather than in the usual often uncomfortable triangle between client and contractor, others were looking specifically at the possibility of providing a total technical and professional package to clients. The rapidly increasing technological demands of construction in the second half of this century have meant that architects on almost every project of any size have to work with structural and services engineers and consultants, as well as quantity surveyors and landscape architects. The complexities and imperatives of site construction have encouraged specialization in contract administration which itself has beome increasingly complex in its own special development of the law.

Engineers like Sir Ove Arup and Sir George Grenfell Baines have been in the forefront of establishing large multi-disciplinary practices encompassing all the design and technical expertise a client is likely to need for any project from building a hydro-electric dam to a hotel or university campus. So influential has this approach to design practice been that some years ago Arup's protégé Edward Happold, an engineer and not an architect, was appointed head of a school of architecture.

All of this is only an extension of the Modern Movement concept played out by Le Corbusier in particular, of the architect as leader of the design team. However, commonly it is the architect's role as leader of the team that is under threat. Not only are some of the largest multi-disciplinary practices engineer-led, but increasingly, the architect's right and competence to lead are being challenged.

For decades architects have grumbled about the problems of management: office management; practice management; project management; construction management; financial management; and whilst they have grumbled, attended the odd short course and muddled along, others have prepared themselves to fill the gap. Commercial clients speak the language of finance, management and the law and like most people respond well to those that speak the same language. Large contractors are in the business of construction management and economics, and respond well to those that understand their business.

During the early stages of gaining large contracts architects usually find that teams are put together with representatives of all those consultants who are likely to be required to execute the job, if won. Many consultants, architects included, give this job-getting role a high priority and deploy specialist personnel and partners to take care of it. In a high powered job-getting team, everybody wants to leave the least possible element to chance and to use the skills available to maximum benefit: the architect may well find that designing and drawing are left to him, but in many cases, chairing and minuting meetings, preparing presentations and other 'marketing' strategies, and client liaison, are all just as likely to be carried out by others, according to their skills rather than their job titles.

Just as the demands of the market have become more varied and specialist, so have the controls imposed by government agencies. Concerns with public health and safety, with energy conservation and the general quality of the public domain, have all given rise to a dizzying tide of construction controls, regulations and standards, with which the architect must comply. Considerable time and effort is devoted in the architect's office to establishing the correct standards for a product and ensuring compliance. In Europe the situation is currently complicated by the need to standardize the standards. This is a painful process for most and can lead to curious anomalies, but ultimately should enable all design professionals to operate with ease across Europe. Clients who commonly already work across national frontiers will know that the product they receive in Naples is of a comparable performance standard to that produced in Nottingham or Nantes.

Hi-tech future

Whilst architects have to operate in the business world of today, they find it increasingly attractive and helpful to use the benefits of modern technology in their work. A great deal of the work of architects remains graphic, from the initial sketch design for a project, through the communication of design ideas to other members of the team and the production drawings that guide the constructors. It is only a few decades since architects were primarily working with pencils or variable thickness pens on treated linen sheets. In the meantime, a whole plethora of plastic films for drawing on have followed the introduction of high-quality tracing paper. Constant line pens become ever more refined and are probably now at the limits of their sophistication, except where they are further developed for use in computer plotters. For even the smallest office now generally has some computer graphics capability. Larger offices are equipped with large and sophisticated computer equipment which can produce everything from optional viewpoint perspectives to production drawings. There are architects' offices now without drawing boards at all. The workers sit at computer terminals inputting information from their own small screen to the mainframe machine, which then delivers the final drawing plotted at any scale on sheets that can be as large as any previously delivered from the drawing board.

The development of computer aided design (CAD) and other computer techniques has particularly strengthened the position of the small practice that can afford essential equipment. Apart from design and drawing aids, architects can use software to calculate costs, or structural requirements, lighting and heating requirements and so on. Using FAX and telex, and computer links, consultants can instantly pool and exchange information. The desk-top publishing facilities available on comparatively cheap micro-computers help the smaller practice to publish reports and other documents of a very high quality of presentation, without the need to employ ancillary staff, specialists or outside consultants.

The ability of the construction industry in many countries to get on with the job of small works without the aid of architects has meant that the future of small-scale community-based general practice is very limited. Unlike medical general practitioners, architects are bound to compete for work against their more powerful colleagues. However, given the benefits of modern technology, there is little doubt that the sole practitioner is likely to enjoy a new and longer lease of life, provided he or she offers not just efficiency, but a design product properly marketed to the right clients. Large practices are almost without exception established multi-national operations. The price of their multi-disciplinary and hi-technology power is an insatiable requirement for work to pay salaries and bills. Whether multi-national corporations employing multi-national, multi-disciplinary building production consultants improve the environmental quality of the world is another question.

CHAPTER 8

Making buildings

THERE are certain times when we are particularly conscious of buildings. Sometimes these moments are associated with a major event in our lives: perhaps our first day at a new school or college, when we are married or taken to hospital, when we start a new job, or look around for the last time as we retire from one. In such cases, and there are many in the lives of everyone, it is often the event that has the greater impact; the building provides the setting. We like to feel that the setting is appropriate to the event though, and would feel disconcerted by a wedding ceremony that took place in an operating theatre.

There are also specific stages in life when our involvement in a building goes beyond its (by no means unimportant) function as a background: when, in particular, we decide to buy a property. It might be a workplace, even a factory, that we want to obtain, but for the majority of us it is the purchase of a house which presents us with the greatest problems and, psychiatrists tell us, often creates a time of very great stress. Certainly, for those who are in a position to put a 'down payment' on a house and are prepared to commit themselves to years of paying off a mortgage, the choice has to be 'right'. A house is likely to be the most expensive purchase that most people in the West who are fortunate enough to be able to do so will ever make. Few embark upon the adventure lightly.

Naturally, what are considered to be the most important factors when buying a house will differ from one purchaser to another: for some it may be its position and 'a good address'; for others it may be the look of the building, whether it seems modern, or homely or inviting. Estate agents will tell us that it is the fittings of the kitchen or the luxury of the bathroom that sells houses. To some extent this may be true, but most people also choose houses for the number and size of the bedrooms and reception rooms, their suitability for the furniture they may own, the safety of the stairs, the ease of running the home, the potential of the garden, the addition of a garage, the possibility of having a workshop or greenhouse – and other factors that affect their families and accommodate their interests. Similar considerations influence the choices made by the owners of businesses or the managers of companies, the shareholders and directors of stores, theatres, hotels, restaurants and service industries when buying, renting or building property: the premises must match, as far as possible, the needs and values of the intending owners and occupiers.

After the purchase alterations are undertaken, redecoration is done to suit new tastes, carpets are laid and furniture arranged, the new building becomes 'home'. Before long though, the first flush of excitement passes. The details fade and the daily business of living and working takes over. Except for showing around occasional visitors or playing 'musical rooms' in an office building when new staff are taken on, the building becomes just another part of the general environment. Once in a while it may be noticed, again with surprise and pleasure, but for the most part it is lived in, accepted, neutral.

Until, that is, something goes wrong. A damp spot in the corner, wet rot in a window frame, a leak from the water tank – minor failures that are irritating and sometimes quite expensive to put right, are acknowledged as inevitable. But no one expects the foundations to sink, the walls to bulge, or the roof to slide off. A drying-out crack in the plaster may be tolerated but not one that reveals that the wall is fractured. It is usually accepted that over the centuries some failures are bound to occur. Everyone is familiar with the appeals of churches and cathedrals to rebuild the tower or replace the rotten timbers of an ancient roof. These are indisputable signs of old age to which we respond; appeals to pay for the repair of such weaknesses in buildings of our own time would not induce many people to give generously.

In fact though, we only see the buildings of the past that have survived either through their structural sturdiness in the first instance, or by maintenance and rebuilding over the years; we do not see the buildings or parts of them that have failed or collapsed. When church spires became fashionable in Britain many masons tried their hand at building them. Numerous spires collapsed into the choirs and naves of the churches, just as had over-ambitious towers before them. In France the patrons of ecclesiastical architecture each tried to build the highest cathedral, though the builders were not always technically a match for the structural problems involved. It was not until the 550 foot (168 metres) great tower and the choir vaulting of Beauvais collapsed in an avalanche of stone and dust that their competitiveness came to an end.

With the writing of the treatises on building, like that by Leon Battista Alberti in the mid-fifteenth century, many of the solutions to the problems that 'him I term Architect' might encounter, many principles of structure and rules of building, were defined. Paralleled by the growth of the printing media these treatises became essential to the general training of an architect as the profession emerged. Sometimes building failure, especially as a result of extreme situations such as a major disaster, was a spur to safer and better subsequent building. Thousands of tall, timber-framed and thatched houses packed in the narrow and twisting lanes of medieval London went up in flames on the night of the Great Fire of 1666; the London Rebuilding Act of the following year introduced standards of building and room heights, wall thicknesses and materials which ensured that such an accidental conflagration would never be repeated. Many laws and by-laws followed, leaving a legacy of legislation that remains with us.

An architect today must acquire a broad knowledge which ranges from the theory of structures on the one hand, to the current Building Regulations on the other. He is required to design within constraints that the physical and man-made laws impose, in the interests of the safety and overall protection of his clients. In doing so he must, in Alberti's words, 'by sure and wonderful Art and Method' be able with 'Thought and Invention, to devise and, with Execution, to compleat all those works' which can, 'with the greatest Beauty, be adapted to the Uses of Mankind'.

To build in truth

Professor C. Bernal, eminent in science if not in architecture, once remarked to a gathering of architects that the only requirement of a building as far as he was concerned was to stop his papers from being blown about. Walls would do that; presumably he would have had a few further remarks to make if his papers had been soaked by the rain coming from above. Of course, his provocative comment was intended to draw attention to the fact that the first purpose of building is to serve very basic functions of protection and sheltering, however much architects may agonize over the aesthetics of design.

Although the technology of architecture may be very complex most of it revolves around two fundamental issues: how to enclose space, and how to span space. Enclosure can be achieved by wind-defeating, not to say enemy-resisting, walls, whether they are around a city, such as Jericho or York, or around a citadel like Avebury Rings or Great Zimbabwe. But to keep the rain out, to provide protection from winter snows or scorching sun, a space defined by walls needs to be spanned by a roof. This immediately exerts constraints on the size and shape of the space to be covered; tree trunks or stone slabs laid horizontally from wall to wall and without further support, behave differently.

While timber is a 'tensile' material with sufficient elasticity to take the strain, stone is a 'compression' material, capable of resisting considerable vertical pressure, but with very little elasticity. A loaded beam is under compression forces on its uppermost side, and is in tension on its underside. Whether it is an oak beam or a stone one the forces exerted are of similar kind. Both are subject to the same kinds of gravitational forces, the same 'loads' of wind velocities or moving people on upper floors, as any other material doing the same job. But although stone may be a stronger material for building walls that will exploit its compression strength, the tensility of timber makes it more suitable as a spanning material. The principles, the physical 'laws' that govern the properties and the behaviour of different structures are the same the world over. But the availability of certain materials, their suitability for the specific task, their permanency and resistance to rot or decay, their latent heat and warmth or coolness in different climates, their susceptibility to working and shaping of details, and their aesthetic appeal according to the values of the place or times – all these factors help determine their selection.

In a sense the history of building technology could be unfolded in terms of man's struggle to cope with the requirement for bigger buildings, unimpeded volumes, wider spans, more floors, easier circulation, better lighting and services, while meeting the perennial demands for greater economy of materials, effort and expense. Such a linear view of building technology would be as simplistic as one based on 'style', and at odds with the fact that many societies have not felt the same needs, nor had the same priorities in building. Nevertheless, some measure of technological 'progress' can be identified, especially if the influence of different architectural traditions upon each other is recognized.

Necessity may not always be the mother of architectural invention: prestige often is too, as the architect endeavours to satisfy the requirement that special uses should be matched with appropriate buildings. Such uses may not always relate to the accommodation of man's physical or mental comfort; in the creation of suitable arenas for religious rites, or the demonstration of political power and authority, the common man or woman may be positively intimidated by architecture. Private passions and public enterprise, sacred duties and military might have provided the motivation for countless buildings wherein comfort has played relatively little part, but in which mystery, grandeur and authority have been of great importance. Enveloping space, relative scale and enrichment of detail have often combined to create architecture that is awe-inspiring – and sometimes inspirational too.

If these demands have led builders to structural innovations in order to solve them, they have none the less worked with craftsmen whose techniques, skills and tools have remained remarkably constant over the centuries. Modern carpenters and joiners would recognize and be able to work with the tools of their Roman counterparts, and though the adze has been discarded they employ today the chisel, auger, toothed saw and plane of medieval woodworkers. Builders in stone work with tools that have changed little from Norman times. For centuries the Guilds protected the interests, the secrets and 'mysteries' of the crafts, set standards and ensured the passing on of skills by a rigorous system of prolonged apprenticeship. Master masons jealously guarded their 'templets', with which they traced on plaster floors, like the one that survives at Limoges, the shapes of their favoured mouldings. But they had to modify and improve their methods as buildings became more sophisticated, classical details required greater precision, and new materials such as stucco were increasingly specified.

Conservatism in the building crafts, and the persistence in the use of particular materials has meant that change in building form and function may often be achieved with traditional means. For instance, though Roman builders had used fired brick in Britain, it disappeared with their departure. Reintroduced by Huguenot refugees from the Netherlands, its versatility as a material was seen first in the country houses of the wealthy. Masons frequently became bricklayers, often cutting the brick to the mouldings they had been accustomed to carving in stone. The continuation of the forms developed in the working of one material may often be seen in the handling of the material that superseded it. Greek temples, though built in stone, bear all the evidence of having been based on the construction of former wooden temples that have perished.

When, in the nineteenth century, structural ironwork was used on an extensive scale, it was frequently with the details cast in imitation of stone technology. The new material, seen at its best today in the great mid-century railway termini, presented considerable aesthetic problems to the Victorian engineers and architects. No building complex demonstrates this more clearly than St Pancras Station in London, built between 1868 and 1874. Its immense train shed roof, with iron arches spanning 243 feet over the platforms, was designed by the engineer W. H. Barlow; before it, but visually totally unrelated to it, stands the opulent St Pancras Hotel, designed in eclectic Italian Gothic style by the architect Sir George Gilbert Scott, as extravagant in its use of stone and terra-cotta detailing as Barlow's shed is functionally austere.

Much of the dilemma of architecture is the satisfaction of functional requirements, through the potential and constraints of structures, while achieving buildings of quality. 'Design with Beauty; Build in Truth' declares the encircling ribbon around the youthful architect and mason in Walter Crane's 'Arts and Crafts' heraldic motif for the Architectural Association. As we are all aware, beauty lies in the beholder's eye. It lies in the designer's as well, and the two do not always share the same vision, nor the same emotional responses to form: the architect may well design with beauty according to his lights and still not satisfy the tastes of others. Building 'in truth' is often interpreted as 'truth to materials' – not forcing them to behave in ways inappropriate to their character. That, in the words of John Keats (from which the slogan above was derived), 'Beauty is truth, truth beauty', is probably not denied by architects, but few use either word these days to define their role. They are happier with the other two words in the injunction: 'Design' and 'Build', hoping, perhaps, that beauty and truth will be the outcome of informed design and competent construction. Nevertheless, it does not necessarily follow that a building that fully satisfies its functional demands is an object of beauty: a bomb shelter or a gasometer might be ideal for its job without having much aesthetic appeal. The problems of the dialectic between the material and the abstract, between function and aesthetic became even greater as the industrial age advanced.

In fact these problems have continued since that time to be ever more complex, as both the use of materials and constructional methods have become more complex to meet our ever more sophisticated demands on buildings.

Making and the makers

The revolutionary iron and glass 'train sheds' of the nineteenth century were just that, open-ended sheds filled with smoke and steam, but protecting passengers from rain and snow. They were remarkable in their time for their large clear spans and the lightness of their skeletal structure, both in engineering and experiential terms. In the late twentieth century, not only have we banished the noxious exhalations of the steam locomotive from our stations, but we have little time for cover, without a controlled internal environment, in any enclosed space.

The history of technological development in the making of buildings over the past century or so has been centred on these two primary concerns: first, making bigger buildings to meet the new accommodation requirements of the industrial and post-industrial ages, and secondly, the extension of our powers of environmental control within the spaces that we create.

In tackling both these concerns in the making of buildings engineers have contributed as much if not more than architects. There was a time in the latter half of the nineteenth century when the technological *and* artistic/creative skills of the engineer seemed far more accomplished and progressive than those of a tired style-mongering architectural profession: 'Perhaps the most regrettable weakness of English architects at the present time', suggested architect and writer George Kerr, to an audience of architects in 1884, 'is their want of that higher scientific skill which they allow engineers to monopolise.'

It was just this sort of 'division of labour' that Hermann Muthesius's 'Deutscher Werkbund' of 1907 was set up to counter, by bringing together leading representatives of the arts, crafts, trades and industry to achieve high quality industrial art. The Berlin electricity giant AEG appointed the architect Peter Behrens as design consultant in 1907, and in this role he not only designed cookers, radiators, lamps and the firm's catalogues and stationery, but their showrooms and factories as well, including the famous Turbine Factory of 1908–9. Muthesius, an architect, was strongly influenced by his years as cultural attaché to Germany's London embassy from 1896 to 1903, and the Werkbund was a successor to the ideas of William Morris and his followers, but with the important difference that members of the Werkbund were committed to the exploitation of technological and industrial advance rather than pre-industrial craft skills and practices. The influence of the Werkbund reached far into the new century, especially through its exhibitions of 1914 and 1927, which included work by men such as Ludwig Mies van der Rohe, who in 1927 was a vice-president of the Werkbund, and Walter Gropius, later founder of the Weimar Bauhaus.

Before the Werkbund was established in Germany, England was importing building technology from across the Atlantic: in 1904 Mewes and Davies constructed the Ritz Hotel in London using a steel frame. Concrete was an altogether more European technology, with the French in the forefront with the work of François Hennebique and Auguste Perret in particular. But the expressive use of concrete in Europe also owed much to the 'new world', as demonstrated by the dubbing of Karl Moser's 1926 church of St Antonius in Basle *Seelensilo*, or 'Silo of the Souls', referring to the then current interest in the rugged forms of the grain silos of the American mid-west. Both types of framed construction permitted the development of deeper plan, higher buildings, than those employing 'traditional' load-bearing techniques. At the same time, the use of a structural frame meant that the outer walls of the building did not necessarily have to carry major loads, and could therefore be lighter and more transparent.

Medieval timber-frame buildings had long ago demonstrated the freedom that a structural frame gave in terms of fenestration, but the new steel and concrete frames were pulled behind the exterior of the building with the thin 'curtain' wall drawn across the exterior. The Admiralty engineer G. T. Greene built a stunning building early on the path to curtain walling, as early as 1858: the Sheerness boat store has an iron frame with continuous bands of glazing and corrugated iron infill panels on the façade. By 1918, Willis Polk had built the Hallidie Building in San Francisco, which had a fully glazed non-load bearing curtain wall. From now on the architect had almost unlimited freedom in the expression of building façade, regardless of the structure behind.

By this time, the architect had the full panoply of modern technology at his disposal to achieve a completely controlled environment within the glazed skin. Air conditioning had been proposed in the 1830s, by the chemist and physician David Boswell Reid, for Sir Charles Barry's new Palace of Westminster, though it was to be fifty years before the use of electricity for forced ventilation was to make it a truly practical proposition. The passenger elevator was pioneered by E. G. Otis in the early 1850s, and the electric incandescent light bulb had been invented in 1879. The combined potential of framed construction and environmental control, made possible the Modern Movement objective of a truly 'international style'.

As the elements of structural and environmental engineering in buildings have become more complex, the design has become as much a team activity as the construction. Architects have continued to take a lead in artistic expression in buildings, even celebrating many functional aspects, like Louis Kahn in his Medical Research Building for the University of Pennsylvania, or Norman Foster's Renault building which offers delight in the display of its elegant structure. In Foster's work we may see a parallel with the work of the nineteenth-century engineers, where unadorned structural display was all the art required. Yet with much 'hi-tech' architecture there is always the doubt that the technological display is too contrived for its own sake, rather than being the result of rational functional requirements. This charge has been levelled at Behrens' turbine factory, and one might be forgiven for wondering whether the Oxford ice skating rink actually warrants its dominant masts and guys.

Living systems

We began this chapter with a consideration of our attitudes to the buildings that form our homes, and it is interesting to return to these 'traditional' domestic buildings now. For this is both what most of us seem to want, and how we perceive what we have: 'traditional homes'. There are tired old jokes about modernist architects living in Georgian town houses, or half-timbered country houses, but what may be true of architects seems certainly to be so for the rest of us. We may admire modern paintings and sculpture, music and literature, but we crave the familiarity and comfort of old domestic forms in which to raise our families and to take our ease.

This has resulted in England, since the mid-nineteenth century, in the consistent development of 'neo-vernacular' and 'neo-Georgian' houses for the people. From the 'Tudorbethan' 'semi' of the inter-war suburbs, so neatly parodied in Sir Osbert Lancaster's

Homes Sweet Homes, to the pseudo Essex vernacular of current 'design guide' speculative housing, the almost universal approach to the design of private housing has embodied an aping of historic 'traditional' forms. Chastened by the building and social failures of modernist public-sector housing, even government development agencies returned in the mid 1970s to the development of cottage homes, after almost half a century dominated by tower blocks and megastructures.

We will not debate here the appropriateness of the forms, but rather, look for a moment at just how 'traditional' this housing is. For, as we have said, our expectations of buildings now are much more sophisticated than they were 100 or 150 years ago.

After the First World War, the British Government was committed to providing 'homes fit for heroes', to mitigate the appalling shortage of decent working-class housing in the country, and some would say, to quell any thoughts of revolution in the minds of a dissatisfied population looking towards recent events in Russia. The powerful influence of the Garden City movement and some of its leading protagonists at the time, ensured that the form of this new housing was based on a reinterpretation of the idealized cottages of the pre-industrial artisan. But war had left the country with very depleted supplies of traditional materials and skills. There were few bricklayers and fewer bricks, and similarly few tilers and tiles, plasterers, and so on. Architecture, and maybe society, called for solid recognizable homes, but the traditional means to meet the scale of task were not to hand.

The result was a short period of intensive innovation, which though soon over, left both the construction of most housing changed and created a context for further gradual development and change which has continued to the present day. Rendered cottages with slate roofs were built, which were actually built of steel frames and other components, using the skills and materials of the war-time shipyards; 'stone' cottages were built, using site-manufactured concrete blocks, with the internal walls rubbed smooth with pumice to obviate the need for plaster and plasterers; and on St George's Plateau, in the centre of Liverpool, a demonstration house was built in a matter of days, which looked just like a brick-built neo-Georgian villa. In fact, the main structure of the house was made using the Canadian 'Dominion', timber-frame system, with fibreboard internal wall linings; the brick was only skin deep, to satisfy fire regulations and the aesthetic sensibilities of the architects.

Timber-frame housing has enjoyed considerable success in

England over the past couple of decades. The main advantage to the builder is the one that was demonstrated in Liverpool half a century before: speed of erection. One of the largest cost elements that the developer has to bear in housing is the cost of construction finance, during that period when he has no completed product to sell. The erection of a timber frame can take weeks or even days compared with the months or even a year that it will take before the first brick houses will be complete. Even if timber-frame houses are brick clad, to satisfy a range of prejudices not encountered in the United States, Scandinavia and other parts of the world, the saving in construction time is substantial.

The British building industry has had its problems, however, with the development of innovative building techniques in housing. Many of the more dramatic instances of innovation pursued after the First and Second World Wars ended in equally dramatic failures: in the 1920s some local councils had to demolish steel houses only a few years after they were completed as the structure corroded; similar failures occurred with some of the reinforced concrete systems. But perhaps even more worrying have been the failures resulting from the mismatch between the users' expectations and the performance of some of the less revolutionary innovations.

When we talk of traditional construction, part of the reassurance of the term comes from the fact that we know not only how the building was made, but also what we may or may not do with it, or expect it to withstand. The respectable traditional builder generally only had two options in terms of the quality of construction: to build well or very well. The materials and details had at least to be fit for their purpose or at best of the finest. It is true that much speculative housing of the eighteenth and nineteenth centuries was built by disreputable builders who achieved neither of these qualities. Oxford, for example, still has examples of nineteenth-century housing with external walls only one half-brick in thickness (about 4 inches or 100 mm), and though these have survived, there are documented examples of houses so constructed, collapsing shortly after completion. Regardless of these unprincipled practices, the performance expectation of traditional methods is well understood, supported as it is by centuries of experience in construction and use.

It is easy to see that once we begin a pattern of substantial non-traditional innovation, or prototypical construction, we no longer have this performance experience to rely upon. It is therefore hardly surprising that major innovations sometimes lead to major failures.

Even minor innovations which result in unexpected performance can cause the building user problems, particularly in a domestic situation, where there are no 'experts' responsible for the upkeep of the building. When timber-frame housing started to become very popular again in England in the 1970s, few owners realized that they were living in sophisticated 'non-traditional' housing. After all, from the outside they generally looked like ordinary brick cottages. The less than happy results of cutting holes in external walls for extra plumbing, or problems with fixing sturdy wall shelving, were not therefore anticipated by most owners.

These particular problems have been well publicized, and timber-frame house builders generally now provide purchasers with a guide to the construction of their house. However, many home owners are still caught out by constructional innovation in their own homes, and there is often incongruence between the objectives and attitudes of designers and constructors and users. A recognition of the gaps between the concerns of those who make buildings and those who use them, has led to a more general commitment to the involvement of users in the design and even the construction of buildings.

At Newcastle upon Tyne Ralph Erskine, a British architect who has worked mainly in Scandinavia, maintained a 'surgery' where residents of the Byker area could discuss design issues with him and his team. With their participation nearly 10,000 people were rehoused between 1970 and 1981 in a friendly, enclosed community environment. A similarly democratic approach was adopted by Lucien Kroll at Louvain, Belgium, where university buildings were designed with the participation of both the students who would be accommodated and the workers who built them.

Hermann Hertzberger's insurance headquarters in Appeldoorn in Holland is an outstanding example of user involvement in the design and management of a commercial building. But if we look at the making of domestic buildings we can find an even more telling example. For the self-build timber-frame system devised by the architect Walter Segal was developed specifically to enable people with no traditional building skills to design and build their own homes. This 'non-traditional' system in the process also makes the resident fully conversant with the construction of his or her own home, in a way seldom achieved by 'user manuals' or the researches of even the most committed 'do-it-yourself' enthusiast.

PART III

ARCHITECTURE FOR TODAY

CHAPTER 9

The rise and fall of modernism

ANYONE who has given any thought to modern architecture must have wondered what is meant by 'modern'; after all, surely every style of architecture is modern in its own time. And, one might continue to reflect, if modern simply means the architecture of today, or of this century, then what is 'modern*ism*'? Then again, there is a lot of talk about 'postmodernism', but if 'modern' means 'of today', then how can anything that has already been built be 'postmodern', and how can it be possible to talk about 'postmodern architecture'? There is good reason to be confused by these terms, let alone by all the arguments in favour, or in criticism, of what they stand for.

Even these reflections assume that 'modern' *does* refer to the architecture of today, though in fact, the span of time implied by the term is quite vague. For instance, some eighteenth-century writers made a distinction between 'ancient' and 'modern' as being between the 'classical' (of Ancient Greece) and the medieval (the 'modern'), which they judged to be inferior. In the middle of the eighteenth century, however, there was a remarkable change in attitudes with, notably, a belief in the idea of progress, through 'rationalism' to the ultimate perfection of mankind. This is one of the convictions of the period that relates very closely to some of the underlying philosophical principles of 'modern', or twentieth-century architecture. It justifies an argument that the modern period dates from about the 1750s (and the rationalist theories of Diderot, Voltaire and the *Encyclopédistes*) to the 1950s, when confidence in continuing 'progress' was questioned.

But another view of the modern places its origins about a century later: for example, with the building of Joseph Paxton's so-called 'Crystal Palace' to house Prince Albert's Great Exhibition of 1851, and Philip Webb's 'Red House' for William Morris of 1859. Paxton's structure of steel frame and glass was, in its day, the largest building ever built, yet, by prefabrication of the parts, and the use of a 'module' system of coordinated dimensions it was assembled in four months. Webb's, on the other hand, was in part a product of the 'Gothic Revival', and its forms were largely derived from the vernacular architecture of south-east England. But its asymmetrical L-plan, use of exposed construction and simplicity of detail, and its design 'from the inside to the outside' – that is, with the exterior dependent on the internal arrangement rather than the façade dictating the organization – was very influential. Both could be seen as precursors of the Modern Movement.

Yet so could many other buildings of the subsequent fifty years, such as Henri Labrouste's reading room, in the Bibliothèque Nationale in Paris with its iron-framed book stacks, glass roof and glass brick floors, completed in 1868; or the immense Galérie des Machines, constructed in 1889 for the Paris Exposition by the engineer V. Contamin and the architect C. Dutert, twice the span of the Crystal Palace, and with massive arched frames supported on roller bearings to take up expansion. Webb's innovations had their counterparts too – in the American houses by H. H. Richardson or the ill-fated Stanford White (he was murdered by a jealous husband).

By the end of the nineteenth century the great railway stations and suspension bridges further demonstrated the potential of iron and steel and glass, and large buildings like Victor Horta's Maison du Peuple in Brussels, and H. P. Berlage's Exchange in Amsterdam showed that many lessons had been learned from these. Gradually the demands that a building had to satisfy were being redefined; it was not uncommon for architects, like the American Louis Sullivan, to insist that a building had to *function*. It had to be designed to suit a particular purpose, and its masses, spaces, details would arise from doing this well. This principle became encapsulated in the phrase 'Form follows function'; modern architecture inspired many aphorisms like that. Of course, many buildings exemplified this principle already – the great railway stations like London's Kings Cross, for example. But architects looked to such buildings as evidence of the beauty that can arise from a truly 'functional' building. They were convinced that when functional demands were fully met, beauty would be the inevitable outcome: like a spoon, a farm waggon or, realizing that this was the new 'machine age', like an ocean-going liner or an airplane. The latter were just two of the kinds of practical, but harmonious products of modern times which offered a model to architects. So argued 'Le Corbusier', the arch-priest of the new design religion, in his immensely influential book *Vers une*

Skidmore, Owings and Merrill's John Hancock Center in Chicago (1969), wears the muscle of its steel bracing dramatically on the outside of the building.

The Solomon Guggenheim Museum on 5th Avenue, New York, designed by Frank Lloyd Wright (1943–59). It takes the form of a spiral ramp, entered by elevator from the top.

A dramatic entrance to the Museum of Anthropology at the University of British Columbia, by Arthur Erickson. The forms are inspired by, but do not imitate, those of the massive timber long-houses of the Haida and other Pacific North-West peoples.

Interior of the Burrell Museum by Barry Gasson Associates (1983). The direct use of modern materials and simple forms relates the interior to the parkland outside, providing a natural well-lit setting for the rich range of objects. (Courtesy, Oxford Polytechnic)

Norman Foster's Sainsbury building, designed in 1978 to house the important collections of John and Lisa Sainsbury at Norwich. Aluminium louvres control the side and top lighting. The space frame structure is of elegant proportions. (Courtesy, Oxford Polytechnic)

Designed by Richard Rogers and Renzo Piano (1977) the Centre Pompidou on the Plateau Beaubourg in the Marais, Paris, is a popular tourist attraction. Services and circulation are displayed on the exterior of the building.

High-rise prestigious residential blocks for the wealthy in Bombay. In their shadow are make-shift bustees constructed of scrap materials by urban squatters. Millions live in such dwellings in India's cities.

Geçekondus, or 'mushroom' housing (literally: built overnight) in Ankara, Turkey, where over 70 per cent of the population lives in self-built, but technically illegal housing. Terms for the building of roads and schools are negotiated with the city authorities.

A self-built house on a raft, built by members of the California 'hippie' culture at Sauselito, San Francisco Bay. Large numbers of these homes have been replaced by speculative housing that imitates their form.

A detail of the Watts Towers, built as a personal fantasy by Simon Rodia, a Latin-American immigrant, which takes the form of a sculpture garden. Shells, broken ceramics, toys and other found objects are pressed into the concrete.

Core housing in Nairobi on a site formerly occupied by shanties made from scrap. A self-built house can be constructed in permanent materials around the core which contains cooking, washing and sanitary facilities.

Housing in central Reading designed by Bentley, Hayward, Murrain, Samuels (1985), which attempts to achieve comfortable, safe, urban housing, using forms appropriate to the particular setting.

A section of the 'Wall' at Byker, Newcastle upon Tyne, by Ralph Erskine, showing the balconies and the frames provided for planting and privacy. Members of the community were consulted in the design of housing units.

architecture, which became a bible of 'functionalism'.

In the world of functionalism there was little room for decoration. It is true that the turn of the century witnessed a remarkable flowering of the decorative arts in *Art Nouveau* or *Jugendstil* (the 'Youth Style') which was international in its popularity. Based on natural forms but often fantastic in its applications – like the extraordinary entrances to the Paris Metro designed by Hector Guimard around 1900 – it was exuberant but short-lived. 'Ornament is crime' thundered Adolf Loos at his contemporaries, and soon decoration was regarded as superfluous, detracting from rather than adding to the purity of well-designed and functional architectural forms. And it was certainly true that some very beautiful buildings designed essentially to meet a specific need would have been reduced by ornament, among them the vast twin airship hangars by the French engineer E. Freyessinet. Huge parabolic sections over 200 feet (62.5 metres) high and nearly 1,000 feet (300 metres) long, they were constructed of concrete, in prefabricated 'folded slabs'.

We are so familiar with concrete (and complain about it so much) that we are apt to forget or ignore its remarkable properties when it is reinforced with steel bars; it is, after all, a mix of sand, cement and water which can be poured like thick soup but which sets like . . . well, concrete. Reinforced, it can be used to span considerable volumes and it has immense strength. Poured, it can take on complex forms like jelly in a mould. But the means of reinforcing it, and the technical problems like the meeting of beams, were not solved overnight, and in the 1880s and '90s there was feverish, inventive activity among builders and engineers. Some of the major difficulties were overcome by François Hennebique, who took out many patents on his methods and whose firm was in great demand early in this century. He devised techniques for combining both beam and floor slab, and refined the principles of reinforcement, to construct reinforced concrete frame buildings.

This was an extremely innovative period, and the potential of steel frame structures which had been demonstrated so dramatically, but hardly functionally, by Gustav Eiffel in his cloud-piercing Parisian tower, was the subject of much investigation in the United States. There architects were intent on exploiting steel's combination of strength and relative lightness. The Reliance Building by D. H. Burnham and J. W. Root, built in Chicago in 1890, was a mere four storeys high; but fifteen more storeys were added four years later, made possible by the structural strength of the steel frame. But it was only made *practical* by the invention of the elevator, an electrically powered vertically moving room that made immediate access to the highest floors available to every office secretary.

Office buildings were comparatively new, especially those such as Frank Lloyd Wright was building with open floors capable of accommodating rows of desks equipped with the new telephones. Not only was there a new emphasis on function, there were also new functions to satisfy: apartment blocks and department stores, insurance buildings and industrial plants. It is not surprising that many of the most adventurous buildings were factories, like the massive, step-profiled chemical works at Luban by Hans Poelzig (1912); or ironically, that designed by Walter Gropius for the making of shoe-lasts for hand-made footwear, the Fagus factory at Alfeld-an-der-Leine, in 1911. Fully exploiting the possibilities of floor slabs supported by columns that were independent of the outside walls, Gropius daringly defined the corners of the building by the meeting of planes of glass. There were many audacious gestures, such as the Fiat works in Turin designed by Matte Trucco, commenced in 1915. It had a race track on the roof, which not only tested the cars but tested the strength, and resistance to vibration, of the huge, flat concrete structure.

Among the most dramatic ideas were those developed in post-revolutionary Russia, but many were too conceptually advanced for the available technology. Vladimir Tatlin's Monument to the IIIrd International, planned to spiral to 1,300 feet with three internal revolving transparent work complexes, not surprisingly never got beyond the model stage. But if many schemes were to remain as architectural fictions, some dramatic Workers' Clubs were designed by Melnikov and Rodchenko. In Russia, at least for the brief but intensely creative period between 1917 and the rise of Stalinism, there was a close relationship between the Constructivist artists and architects. They worked to a common social end, and used the powerful dynamic of shapes, forms, colours and new materials to communicate the spirit of the revolution in art, theatre performance, propaganda graphics and structures.

Art and architecture frequently trod the same path. Some of the German Expressionist artists were trained as architects, but they preferred the immediacy of painting. Expressionist architects, many of them German, endeavoured to match the emotional power of painting in their buildings; Hans Poelzig for example, who designed for the impresario Max Reinhardt a vast 'stalactite cave', the Grosses Schauspielhaus in Berlin in 1919. But the most successful Expressionist building was not designed by an architect at all but by Rudolf Steiner, the founder of Anthroposophy, whose immense 'Goetheanum' at Dornach, Switzerland showed an intuitive grasp of the potential of concrete. In contrast to these ventures in the free forms of Expressionism a few of the Cubist painters had an austere approach to form, calling themselves 'Purists', and among their number was the artist and writer Charles Jeanneret, who became an architect under the pseudonym of 'Le Corbusier'. Some of his houses, like the famous Villa Savoye, were virtually Purist paintings in three dimensions. The more abstract the art form the closer it approximated to architecture. Dutch artists of 'De Stijl' (Style) used the simplest shapes and forms, painted in primary colours, which Gerrit Rietveld employed in his Schroeder House in Utrecht in 1924. These houses sometimes approximated sculpture that could be lived in, manageable at the scale of a house though with some dubious results when translated into larger buildings.

Several major architects of the first half of the century worked out their ideas and often produced their best work in the design of houses. One of these was the Scot Charles Rennie Mackintosh, whose Hill House of 1903 has a certain baronial scale, but also a remarkable use of internal space, with elegant, austere furniture which he also designed. Another was the Finnish architect Eliel Saarinen (father of Eero Saarinen) who designed 'Hvittrask' with his partners at about the same date (1902), a studio-cum-office and dwelling units, on a lake-side west of Helsinki. It shows a clear awareness of the English Arts and Crafts approach. But some were thinking big, dreaming of whole new cities, like the Cité Industrielle planned by the Lyons-born radical Tony Garnier between 1899 and 1918, or the Città Nuova of the Italian Futurist Antonio Sant'Elia (1909–14), who was killed in the First World War. Both these schemes were influential, but neither was built. Nor were Usonia, the limitless pastoral community invented by the eccentric genius Frank Lloyd Wright, or his later endless suburb of Broadacre City. In the American mid-west, which was vast enough for his sprawling communities, he had built several 'prairie houses' which exploited the use of cantilevered concrete floors to open up internal space, and to dissolve the distinction between interior and exterior that traditional load bearing walls emphasized. They would have sat well in Broadacre City. If a number of plans for new cities did not get beyond the drawing board, Sir Edwin Lutyens's grand design for New Delhi, commenced in 1912, certainly did. Planned on an axis which extended from the Viceroy's House to the Friday Mosque in the old city it was imperial in concept, but it skilfully combined Hindu, Mogul and classical details. It was built, he said 'as an Englishman dressed for the climate'.

In *his* urban ideas Le Corbusier owed much to Tony Garnier, but also to the rectilinear 'grid' planning of Manhattan, Chicago and other American cities. His notorious view that a house should be a 'machine for living in' was an argument for a 'mass production house', that would be physically and *morally* healthy, an ideal best expressed in his Dom-Ino and Citrohan house designs. Both names (punning on the game of dominos and the Citröen car) were intended to suggest standardization and efficiency. Essentially low-rise houses as he first conceived them, they were soon reinterpreted in huge apartment blocks, raised on *pilotis*, or piers, under which acres of cars could be parked, which stretched to the far horizons of the Ville Radieuse. They were not built then either, and nor were his plans for cities like Algiers. In fact, there was a period of many years during which Le Corbusier built very little. But after the Second World War he designed several apartment blocks, like the Unité d'Habitation near Marseilles, which demonstrated his ideas of a city within a building, with high-level corridor 'streets' and an abstract playground roof-scape.

'Less is more' pronounced Mies van der Rohe in another of the architectural aphorisms of the Modern Movement, by which he meant that economy of design (but not necessarily financial economy) and functional simplicity brought aesthetic and technological rewards. An expatriate from Germany, he was welcomed in the United States, where immediately after the Second World War he designed an expensive house for one Dr Farnsworth which was a steel-framed shoe-box of elegant proportions, its glass walls totally transparent. Soon afterwards, his towering apartment blocks on Lake Shore Drive in Chicago established a model of austere but immaculate urban architecture. The dominance of a few eminent figures in CIAM, the Congrès Internationaux d'Architecture Moderne, like Mies van der Rohe and Le Corbusier, had a profound effect on world architecture, their example inspiring a number of good buildings and promoting thousands of imitations of sadly lesser quality: more became less.

It was the spread of high-rise, slab-sided buildings that justified the term 'international style' as countless office towers, apartment buildings, airport hotels and, less prestigiously, mass housing blocks sprang up from Sheffield to San Francisco to Singapore. Concrete-framed or steel-framed, modularized and prefabricated, they shared the same cigarette-carton proportions, and, more than any other type of building brought 'modern architecture' into widespread disfavour. Such buildings are what most people mean when they condemn it, complaining of their anonymity and inhuman scale. For the occupants of many tower blocks built to rehouse millions in the 1950s and '60s, it was impossible to identify with the faceless, characterless buildings where they were expected to live. Moreover, in Britain, where Italian 'system building' was adopted as yet virtually untried, there were both social and structural failures. Corridors became the haunts of muggers, elevators were dangerous or unusable, no one cared for the condition of the communal stairs or the rubbish-strewn 'green spaces' below. The deliberate and official destruction by explosion of the Pruitt–Igoe estate in Chicago and the collapse of part of Ronan Point as a result of an accidental gas leak explosion in London were landmarks on the route to the end of modernism.

But in the post-war period when, for twenty-five years or so, modernism was largely unchallenged, there were many buildings, like the Palazzetto della Sport by the Italian engineer–architect Luigi Nervi, with the pie-crust edge of its eggshell-thin shallow dome supported by hinged concrete Y-frames, that were, in many ways, successful. There were the university buildings, such as those by Louis Kahn at Yale, by Mies van der Rohe at Massachusetts Institute of Technology or the genuinely national architecture of the University of Mexico by Juan O'Gorman and others. The sculptural quality of many modern buildings looked well in campus settings, even though they destroyed the essence of the street in urban contexts.

New materials, new methods of construction, new forms and new demands required new theories, which were necessary in order to master the problems they posed. Some were clearly flawed, like the doctrine of 'truth to materials' which hardly described Mendelsohn's Expressionist Einstein observatory in Potsdam, or Le Corbusier's Villa Savoye, both built of brick masquerading as concrete. Much has been written in recent years of the functional failure of 'functionalist' buildings, it has even been argued that 'form follows failure' rather than function, for failure induces change. But though there are many exceptions, around the world today there are numerous memorable buildings that will remain as testimonies to a period of invention and experiment, and often of achievement, virtually unprecedented in history.

Everyday modernism

We may believe that, but for the fine pieces of *building-as-sculpture* that remain successful in special settings, modernism has been an almost unmitigated disaster in terms of the everyday buildings it produced. However, the Modern Movement did both produce and espouse cultural thinking and ideas that still demand our attention. It is true that the range of these ideas and the dialectic between them and the ideas of modern architecture were almost as varied, confused and structurally flawed as were the buildings themselves, but we have to beware of 'throwing out the humanistic baby along with the deterministic bathwater'.

Most avant-garde movements are as short-lived in their flight in any one direction as the bright butterflies of sartorial fashion. However, the essential ideas of modernism, which coalesced and were fully articulated mostly in the first quarter of this century, have been in circulation since the middle of the last, and though the movement may be discredited and 'fallen' in the minds of many, the forms remain nurtured today by old and young artists at the fringes of the architectural establishment. Why should this be? What is there in modernism that has enabled it, despite all the failures, to remain so persistent an alternative force? Inevitably answers to this question will be if not tentative, then partial.

The greatest successes and failures of modernism in terms of scale and volume of production occurred after the Second World War. The global conflict had been the product of naked nationalism in all things from the ruthless application of the pathetic doctrine of racial supremacy, to the perpetration of one style of 'imperial' architecture for public buildings. The great architects at the poles of the 'free world', in Russia or the United States, were modernists, whose design lineage can be directly traced from the Deutscher Werkbund, and particularly the housing exhibition of 1927 in Stuttgart, on via the meetings of the Congrès Internationaux d'Architecture Moderne, which acted as the 'party political' forum for modernist debate and dictat through until the late 1950s. Of course, most of the modernist masters who were German by birth and training had fled the Nazi persecutions of 'decadent' avant-gardes.

So after the war modernism had not only become truly international, but it was anti-imperialist, and a symbol of freedom and willing cooperation rather than oppression: it was world, rather than national architecture. Across the globe it provided a form of architectural expression that was free of repressive association, an aesthetic form for the future that was easily allied to feelings of hope and the potential of humankind to engineer its way out of its problems, with light, economy and elegance.

The ideas of new democratic communities, first put forward cogently, but gently, by Ebenezer Howard, slipped their architectural mantle of pre-industrial vernacular and assumed that of modernism. In Britain, a new generation of school-trained architects were eager to put into practice the building ideas of Le Corbusier, promulgated by books and the international conferences, which had in their rhetoric the humanistic, egalitarian answers to the United Kingdom's problems of crowded industrial cities, riddled with densely packed, dilapidated and out-of-date housing, inadequate in quantity and quality for contemporary needs.

Modernism had all the answers, and in particular, in the post-war era, seemed to combine rational, technological solutions with an artistic and democratic vision of the future. The town planner and writer Thomas Sharp described Le Corbusier's book *The City of Tomorrow*, first published in 1929, as a 'Stimulating, romantic, often hysterical and never very practical prose-poem on the big city of the future', and it was this combination of qualities which made the look irresistible to the form-givers of the 1950s.

The concrete system-building techniques which came to be almost exclusively associated with the modern forms of mass housing that characterized this universal realization of the city of the future, extended pre-war technology in a way that was justified by the seemingly unquenchable demand for new housing. Though the forms were usually undeniably Corbusian, the ideas of the standardized *existenzminimum* (subsistence minimum) dwelling had been fully explored in Germany and Holland in the 1920s, and in the separation of the pedestrian from the car in the influential planning of Radburn, New Jersey, by Clarence Stein in 1928. Pevsner, writing in 1959 in the *Architectural Review* about London County Council's new Roehampton Estate, even suggested that the use of these forms in their landscaped setting was entirely in keeping with the English domestic tradition of houses and villas set in parkland.

The failure of all this has been well documented. During the 1950s and 1960s, working-class communities were fragmented by redevelopment with little thought to the consequences. Planners and architects sought to provide the environments for new communities to grow, using alien forms in existing urban areas, and dispersed and ill-serviced cottage developments, on most of the post-war 'new town' development sites. These new towns generally had inadequate and slowly developing centres that employed concrete modernism for their form, even where the surrounding housing was more traditionally low-rise and brick. With hindsight we can easily appreciate the folly of all this. We must similarly regret that architects, often with little development experience, were so readily convinced of the merits of modernist forms, and so able to convince public policy-makers of their merits too.

Much of the failure of modern architecture and town planning is rooted in a lack of understanding by the public and private sectors of the limitations each has in its operations in a nominally free society. A great deal of the richness that we crave in our cities is simply the product of individual activity within the context of the prevailing market forces. Modernism espoused grand planning approaches only previously employed by absolutist monarchies. The scale of the results is staggering. The failure of 'public modernism' in the immediate post-war decades has given way to a commercial multinational modernism in the 1970s and '80s. This modernism has made the distinguishing of one American city sky-line from another a task only for the cognoscenti, and even more alarmingly has similarly homogenized the cityscape of major urban centres across the world. National imperialism has given way to the imperialism of Western capital.

Not surprisingly, urban environments increasingly dominated by mute, glazed, curtain-walling and featureless dirty grey concrete, where an art gallery may be mistaken for a fire-station, have led to a rising tide of dissatisfaction from those who have to live in and use cities. After nearly half a century of architecture where less was considered more, it is equally unsurprising that less should have become a bore (to paraphrase both Mies van der Rohe and Robert Venturi), and that consequently people should crave form and detail to which they can relate. Perhaps almost equally, we were overdue for a stylistic change.

The architecture critic Ada Louise Huxtable, quotes Clarence Stein: 'The planner's shield should be a simple device – a question mark. . . . When an idea becomes conventional, it is time to think it through again.' In 1983, Michael Thompson described the results he had achieved by setting architectural students the essay title 'Compare Mole's house in "The Wind in the Willows" with Le Corbusier's machine for living'. He observed: 'A few years ago, when the Modern Movement was still in full flood, there was no problem – strike out strongly for Corbusier – but now, with the rise of neo-vernacularism, of self-build, of postmodernism, of public participation, and of the autonomous house, perhaps Mole should be seen as the attractor?' Even given the decline of modernism, the would-be architects found it difficult to commit themselves in print to 'the *unruly local bricolage*' of Mole, rather than Corbusier. One student wrote: 'Though Mole's house appears very attractive from a purely human point of view, I feel that, as an architect, I must side with Corbusier.' As Thompson says: 'In struggling to reconcile his [i.e. the student's] personal aesthetic convictions with his ambition to join the architectural profession he has, unwittingly, excluded architects from the human race.'

Past modernism

Whilst the convention of modernist form is being rejected – and the process is yet far from complete – we are offered what Charles Jencks has called 'a series of discontinuous movements' in its place. It is not surprising that one of the methods that Jencks uses consistently to interrogate these manifestations of style is the test for *multivalence*: complexity in architecture is good, whereas simplicity, or unity is bad. The *postmodernist* movements which Jencks examines are linked by this quality of multivalence in the mind of the critic, and also by their creative association with modernism. For there is no doubt that 'postmodernism' can be clearly separated from both neo-rationalism, which in the work of Leon Krier, Aldo Rossi and others picks up from the work of Heinrich Tessenow, Gunnar Asplund and others, and the new historicism, notably represented by the work of Quinlan Terry in England.

Both as a result of its international success and the 'sculpture in the landscape' quality almost universal in the development of modernist solutions, the dominant criticism of the genre has been the 'placelessness' of the environments it generates. In 1958, the social and economic commentator Hannah Arendt wrote of the public realm that it

'gathers us together and yet prevents our falling over each other . . . What makes mass society so difficult to bear is not the number of people involved, or at least not primarily, but the fact that the world between them has lost its power to gather them together, to relate and to separate them. The weirdness of this situation resembles a spiritualistic seance where a number of people gathered around a table might suddenly, through some magic trick, see the table vanish from their midst, so that two persons sitting opposite each other were no longer separated but would be entirely unrelated by anything concrete.

The trick was the development of modern cities with no concern for the vital ordering components of the city – the block and the street. This discontinuity of the town environment has been reinforced by the activities of town planners, who since the birth of their profession early this century, have sought to sanitize urban places by *zoning* buildings and activities – residential, commercial, industrial and so on – in a way that dilutes the richness of form and activity that characterizes our largely unplanned older cities.

Increasingly, the 'Moles' have revolted, seeking an environment with both utility and meaning for their community. At the same time, more and more design professionals have turned to historic environments, usually developed accretively over long periods of time, for inspiration for contemporary architectural problems. The influence on architectural thinking of the discipline of sociology, particularly in the 1960s, has been reinforced in the 1970s and '80s by belated appraisals of user satisfaction with urban environments, brought about by inner city decline and violence.

It is ironic that the solutions of modernism, in so large a part promoted by the visionary artist Le Corbusier, are condemned now for their apparent inhuman rationalism. As a result, it is not just the architectural aesthetes and avant-garde that look for complexity, but community architects, and that group who describe themselves as '*phenomenologists*', who are primarily concerned with the reinforcement by development of a 'sense of place', and typify an approach to life and its works that is at once rational *and* mystical.

In his essay on the use of phenomenology in the design studio, Botond Bognar rejects both what he calls '*productivist rationalism*, which follows the performance principle of positivist science and limits architecture to the aspects of how buildings are constructed and how they work', without centrally addressing the 'human implications and values', and the *'formalistic rationalism*, which restricts architecture primarily to the aspects of how buildings appear visually'. In their place he proposes a phenomenological approach which can 'conceive of the environment as a network of potential places capable of inviting and sustaining a complex of physical, emotional, intellectual, and spiritual interactions'. In furtherance of these objectives, the approach concerns itself primarily with the pursuit of 'spirit of place' or *genius loci*, seen here as synonymous with Christopher Alexander's 'quality without a name', and in no small part dependent on a designed 'multiplicity of the environment'.

The fall of modernism appeared to many to leave a stylistic and philosophical vacuum in terms of the production of buildings. Over the past ten years, a drift to the political right in many countries of the Western world, with the consequent emphasis on the funding of most building programmes by private sector capital, has tended to taint new architectural approaches with the apparent overweening interest of designers for the concerns of their paymasters. 'Commercial' has long been a dirty word for the artist architect. But we should be neither distressed by any move towards greater accountability to client and user by architects, nor a general trend away from 'mass' solutions. And if ever there was a vacuum left after the decline and fall of modern architecture, it has rapidly been filled with a satisfying menu of alternative approaches from the 'hi-tech' of Foster or Rogers, to the postmodern classical of Ricardo Bofill or James Stirling.

CHAPTER 10

Architecture on view

WHEN we regard all those 'tower blocks' and 'slab blocks' of the 1950s and 1960s we can easily believe that the whole of modern architecture has been cast in the same mould. Because so many people are obliged to live in multi-storey apartment blocks, and because so large a number also work in high-rise office buildings, it is really not surprising that many of us feel that these immense structures dominate the cities in which we live. Some of them are remarkable buildings technically, like the Hancock building in Chicago, strapped in diagonal steel bracing to withstand the effects of gale force winds on a structure 1,000 feet high. A whole city of Hancock buildings would be intimidating and monotonous, though such towers are here to stay as long as city centre land values remain so high. Mile-high buildings are technically feasible and may well be built early in the twenty-first century.

Nowadays many architects have become aware that such tall buildings can be dull, and they have designed them with greater variety of profile. One, by Philip Johnson, has a witty – or vulgar, depending on your point of view – Chippendale pediment outlined against the sky. Go to a city like Austin, Texas today, and you can see polychrome, tinted and mirror-glazed blocks standing like chessmen on a great table-top game board. At a distance such sculpturing works, up to a point, while the plane surfaces are ideal for the projection of multi-media sound and light rock shows. But at street level, where the pedestrian encounters the building, they are often insensitive or over-scaled. The frequent strictures against modern buildings still apply in these instances.

It is easy to overlook the fact that there are innumerable buildings which, standing in parks or more generously in the urban setting, are far more varied in form. Many of these arise from the specialized demands of the clients, and are among the building types to which architects since the Second World War have made a significant contribution: factories, railroad termini, airports, hospitals, theatres, banks, shopping malls, sports stadia, leisure centres are just a few. Among them have been some memorable architecture: who has not seen and remembered photographs of the TWA building (now the John F. Kennedy Terminal) by Eero Saarinen, or the great shells of Jorn Utzon and Ove Arup's Sydney Opera House? From Le Corbusier's intimate chapel of Notre Dame du Haut at Ronchamp, to the spiralling roof of Kenzo Tange's Olympic Stadium in Tokyo, from Moshie Safdie's 'Habitat' housing megastructure at Montreal to Norman Foster's Hongkong and Shanghai Bank, a succession of dramatic, formally stimulating and often aesthetically satisfying buildings has been designed and built all over the world. There are far too many for us to summarize them here; better perhaps, to consider just what has been achieved within one broad category.

Where, some people ask, are the modern equivalents of the great cathedrals of the past? One might well counter with the question, where are the great congregations of the past? Architecture alone cannot create them. But which are the buildings that today can draw in the public, that can inspire them or fill them with awe, or which provide an appropriate setting for contemplation, if not worship?

Cabinets of curiosities

We noted in Chapter 1 the speech made by the Prince of Wales in which he likened the winning competition entry for the proposed extension to the National Gallery in Trafalgar Square to 'a carbuncle on the face of an old friend'. But the faces of old friends do not have to be beautiful, and Wilkins's National Gallery, a product of nineteenth-century routine classicism, is bland but dull. Prince Charles's intervention, and the exception that he took to the design, forced an inquiry and the eventual loss of the commission. Richard Burton, one of the firm of architects (ABK) who were the target of the Prince's shafts, warned other designers: 'Don't enter for competitions – you might win.' When the dust had settled the American prophet of 'post modern' neo-classicism, Robert Venturi, was invited to take on the commission. Promising 'harmony and analogy' he was delighted to accept and there have been few who have complained about the final choice of architect.

Museums and art galleries undoubtedly arouse much popular

interest, not only because they house the treasures of our past and the icons of the present, but also because they become the focus of so much of our culture. We visit them expecting to be uplifted, stimulated and entertained. They enshrine our heritage and our values, serving many if not all the functions of the ecclesiastical buildings of history: they are the cathedrals of a secularized society. So we expect them to be special buildings. On the whole, architects have risen to the challenge they present. Museums, anyway, have many aspects that are attractive to the architect. They are 'one-offs', so that each museum is a new problem, unlikely to be repeated. They are a public focus, with thousands of people using them every day. They are generally in the trust of directors and staff who are professionally interested in presenting their contents to the greatest advantage, so they tend to be used sympathetically. Elements of design that are important to the architect, such as circulation, spatial volumes, vertical movement, lighting, external and internal finishes, fittings and so on are given high levels of attention. As space does not permit discussion of all the types, styles and problem solutions that architecture represents today, museum and gallery design will serve as an example of its diversity

One of the first major museums of the post-war years was designed by the septuagenarian Frank Lloyd Wright for Solomon R. Guggenheim (1944–59). Facing Central Park, it has the form of an inverted, truncated cone, with an asymmetrical rotunda to one side. The cone expresses the guiding principle behind the design, an immense cantilevered spiral ramp which descends from the elevator tower around an impressive, light-filled hall. There are no sharp interruptions to the flow of space, which 'organically' relates to the smooth, curving forms. Wright himself compared the concrete surface to an eggshell (cartoonists tended to compare the whole building with a Kenwood mixer). It was a remarkable, highly original building in which Wright, typically, showed no acknowledgement to anyone. But it presents problems: the curving walls are not ideal for hanging pictures on, while the descending spiral means that frames are never parallel to the floor plane. An undoubted masterpiece epitomizing Wright's theories, the Guggenheim turns its back on the relentless grid of New York avenues. A sculpture in itself, it now has a defence committee of 'Guggenheim Neighbors' which is opposed to plans to build a slab-block extension designed by Gwathmey Siegal to accommodate the considerable, undisplayed reserve collection.

We are used to seeing imposing, nineteenth-century Classical Revival museums dominating the sides of public squares like ducal palaces. The Oakland Museum in California represents a very different approach to the museum in the city. It is truly urban, flanked by roads, but visitors are invited to enjoy it as a park even when the galleries are closed. Designed in 1961–8 by Kevin Roche and John Dinkeloo, former associates of Eero Saarinen, it consists of three museums in one, built on three levels in a gentle cascade, each floor opening on to gardens landscaped by Geraldine Scott on the roof of the floor below. The Oakland Museum thus combines natural planting with urban formalism. Another modern museum, the Louisiana Kunstmuseum (named after the original owner of the site who married three women all named Louise), was designed in 1958 by Jorgen Bø and Vilhelm Wohlert. It is situated in the park of an old country house 20 miles north of Copenhagen, and close to the sea. A glass corridor across the gardens links the old house with the new, low building. Louisiana comprises a succession of spaces, some closed, some side-lit, some lit from a 'lantern' level above. White-washed brick walls inside and out, exposed timber joists and wood-strip ceilings have a warm quality. Among the trees, and with its pool and stepping stones, the building offers a domestic rather than an institutional setting, not only for paintings and sculpture but for concerts, films and children's clay modelling too. The same architects designed further galleries in 1971 and 1982, as carefully landscaped as their first.

Though such museums largely present a general collection of paintings, sculpture and artefacts, many are required to display objects of a more specialized nature. The working list of the 'Art and Architecture Thesaurus' identifies some *eighty* types of museums and galleries, displaying collections that range from numismatic and philatelic to ethnological and commercial. There are museums of dance and photography, of industry and dentistry, textiles and minerals, not to mention waxworks, herbaria and halls of fame. It is immediately apparent that the requirements of a doll museum, such as the one in Yokohama designed by the offices of Kagawa and Sakakura Sekkei (1987), are quite different from those for a Museum of the Moving Image (London, Avery Associates, 1988) and that both are very different from one which shelters something as unique as the salvaged Tudor warship the Mary Rose.

In the 1960s Canadian architect Arthur Erickson was invited to design the Museum of Anthropology at the University of British

Columbia on a headland site overlooking Vancouver. The collection is of Haida, native American, art from the Pacific north-west, including massive house-posts and totem poles, as well as masks and hand rattles. Without in any way imitating the forms of a Haida community house, Erickson evoked its scale and massive construction with a succession of concrete post-and-beam spans. Between them curved tinted skylights illuminate the interior, which progressively gains in scale and culminates in an immense hall capable of taking the highest totem poles. One side is wholly glazed and looks out on an external park where totems stand before full-scale replica Haida houses. Immensely popular with the Indians, who consider it their museum, it has an expanding collection and a research and conservation area to one side. Here, the entire reserve collection is on view and visitors may add to the growing data on the artefacts. That it is so popular is very largely due to Erickson's sensitivity to the traditional sense of space, and his respect for the impressive artefacts that the museum contains.

It is not merely a matter of scale, though that is important, it is also a problem of 'view'; to be able to study both sides of a medal, while ensuring its safety, presents quite a different problem from displaying airplanes and space-craft while ensuring the safety of visitors. This was the challenge confronting the firm of Hellmuth, Obata and Kassabaum when they designed the National Air and Space Museum on the Mall in Washington, DC in 1972. A row of plain blocks pierced only by 'letter-box' clerestory lights is linked by fully glazed display halls. These are spanned by tubular steel trusses from which the aircraft hang; each intersection of the web of trusses can take a load of 8,000 lb (3,630 kg). The interiors are simple but dramatic, though many people have not been happy with the military precision of the blocks.

Every museum raises particular problems for the designer. Some of these are related to getting objects for display in and out of the building, to storing them, or to providing facilities for research and conservation. Artefacts have to be protected from damage, accidental or malicious; they have to be secure and safe from fire or flood. But many are extremely delicate and can be adversely affected by high humidity, or excessive dryness of the atmosphere. Temperature and humidity differ greatly from one part of the world to another, often from one season to another, demanding skilful environmental control. Lighting presents a perennial problem: direct daylight can be damaging to fabrics and paper, indirect light may not penetrate sufficiently; artificial light can change the colours of objects, shadows can dramatize them or obscure them; surfaces can reflect, absorb or scatter light, and most artificial systems generate heat and running costs.

These are technical issues that must be dealt with by the architect, even though the visitor may be wholly unaware of it. Fortunately, there is trade and professional assistance. But the architect still has to select from a great range of products to meet the specific circumstances for which he is designing. There are, of course, important matters of security to be met, while the accommodation of staff and the provision of services like restaurants and toilets are essential. And most important these days, bookstalls and souvenir shops must be given prominence without hindering the circulation of visitors.

Some would argue that artificial light can be more effectively employed if natural lighting is excluded, while a multi-level building can only be naturally lit from above by an atrium. They were not fashionable when the Hayward Gallery on the South Bank of the Thames in London was designed by the Architects' Department of Greater London Council. The clients were the Arts Council who required five galleries and three outdoor sculpture courts, as well as loading bays, ample storage and plant rooms, passenger and service lifts. The resulting building, executed in *brut* (or rough) concrete, was a complex of levels and trays, concrete sculpture courts with splayed parapets at roof level and a prickly array of pyramidical lanterns against the skyline. Opened in 1968 as the Arts Council flagship, it has been host to many exhibitions – including major ones devoted to architects Sir Edwin Lutyens and Le Corbusier – but its 'brutalist' aesthetic has not endeared it to the public, and its inflexible spaces, fixed ramps and central service towers have not pleased exhibition organizers.

Many gallery directors like the freedom to design new displays with the minimum of fixed installations. In these circumstances a 'well-serviced shed' might be the answer, which is what Foster Associates provided in 1977 for the Sainsbury Centre for Visual Arts at the University of East Anglia. A tubular-steel, space-frame structure provides the support for all the services, the walls and ceiling having virtually identical structures. The frame spans an uninterrupted space 110 feet (33 metres) wide, and both walls and ceiling can admit natural and artificial light through the cladding of adjustable perforated aluminium louvres. What may seem an insensitively 'hi-tech' solution is given classical elegance by its proportions and site.

Whatever its apparent lack of appeal, hi-tech design won many converts with the spectacular popular success of the Centre Pompidou, built in 1977 in the Plateau Beaubourg in the heart of an old quarter of Paris. It was designed by Renzo Piano and Richard Rogers and paid minimal attention to its context; its relation was much closer to the visionary technological dreams of the 1960s Archigram group. Like a lobster, it is an 'exoskeletal' structure but, unlike a lobster, it wears its organs on the outside as well. The immense trusses, manufactured by Krupp, extend to the outer frame which supports the external, transparently covered escalator that snakes up to all levels. From its many vantage points the spontaneous entertainments in the *place* below can be watched. On the east side of the building in a more confined street clusters of service trunking convey a technological imagery, part nautical, part industrial, yet brashly exposed in primary colours. Within, the open spaces are unimpeded, but the exhibition organizers complain that there are no walls on which to hang things, every exhibition must start by designing supports; the clerical staff despair of a vast open plan office in green plastic. But the Pompidou Centre, though it already shows signs of rust, is a popular, even *kitsch* success in its cheerfully anarchic hi-tech audacity.

In the 1980s there has been an unprecedented proliferation in the number of new museums being built. With the onset of the electronic, post-industrial age, nostalgia for the past, a sense of lost innocence, a realization that many craft skills have passed beyond reclamation, and the recognition that the products of the industrial age are often as remote, have all contributed to the demand for new galleries. Awe, and a sense of almost religious wonder have often been replaced by curiosity about the art and artefacts of former generations. To some extent this has been reflected in changing attitudes to architectural design; many lessons have been learned by re-examining the historical record. In some instances this has meant a return to the idealism of the early Modern Movement, its purity and clarity of means, even its white walls. Such was the case with Richard Meier, one of the architects termed 'the New York Five', who shared this view. He designed the new Decorative Arts Museum in Frankfurt.

More than 80 per cent of Frankfurt was destroyed during the Second World War, and its recovery programme, which involved the reconstruction of many historic buildings, also included the design of several museums along the 'Museum Mile' fronting the River Main. The Decorative Arts Museum is situated in the grounds of a nineteenth-century house, the Villa Mezler which, apart from its roof, is a perfect cube with sides of 17.60 metres (57 feet) in length. This dimension Meier echoed in the plan and elevation of his museum. A glass bridge at first floor level links the villa with the new building, whose external cladding in white, porcelain-enamelled steel panels, and quadruple-glazed aluminium framed windows with ventilation regulated by solar sensors, also take their dimensions from the regulating grid of the villa façade.

On plan there is a $3\frac{1}{2}$ degree difference between the axis of the villa and that set by the boundaries of the site. This Meier acknowledged in his design by a subtle overlay of two geometries generated by these axes. They are indicated by the angles of the pedestrian routes. With white cubic pergolas, an open circular sculpture pavilion and a court of trees embraced by the museum wing outside, and with the views offered between the grids of glazing bars and from the ramps between the floors, Meier created a unique relationship between villa, museum and site, and a complex spatial experience, both outside and within. Seven other new museums have risen along the Main – including one where the villa was totally restructured internally whilst retaining its external façades, this the work of Matthias Ungers. Significantly, perhaps, it is designed to house the German Museum of Architecture.

Many architects of the 1980s have reacted against the aesthetic certainties of the modernist period, and have been prepared to look anew, even if with a somewhat quizzical gaze, at the forms, details and symbols of the Western heritage. Many museums of the 1980s have been workshops for new syntheses in design. One of the most successful, pleasing both public and profession, is the Burrell Gallery in Glasgow, designed by Barry Gasson Associates to display a remarkable collection of art treasures. Located in a park, it has been sited with great care to take advantage of the shallow gradient of woodlands and open parkland. The intrusion of its considerable volume has been minimized by a low profile (in fact, it has five storeys inside) and a light-filled perimeter circulation system. The way in which many of the artefacts, even including a medieval doorway, have been incorporated in the structure has delighted visitors, while the attention given to controlled environments for sensitive exhibits has pleased the Burrell curators.

Such museums as these recall the challenge met by the designers of Louisiana or Oakland Museum, in designing with landscape in both park and urban settings. Oblique references to other and earlier buildings may be detected, as in the extraordinary Aerospace Museum in Los Angeles designed by Frank Gehry on an extremely narrow site. It comprises two huge, almost windowless blocks, with a linking glass pavilion, seemingly commenting on the National Air and Space Museum on the Washington, DC Mall, by handling the blocks with dynamic audacity. One inclined block leans over the roadway, while an aeroplane is suspended outside, above the visitor's head.

Meanwhile, on the Washington Mall itself, I. M. Pei's East Building of the National Museum of Art, though block-like on the outside is revealed as a huge, light-filled atrium within, the floors extending like trays into the space, unfolded from the rising escalators. Pei has gone on to other things: his pyramid of glass in the formal Cour Napoleon, the centre court of the Louvre seems outrageous to many Parisians, but stems in part from an acknowledgement of the geometric 'solids' of pure classicism. As daring today as was the Eiffel Tower a century before, Pei's pyramid was designed with the aid of computers and built with a rod and cable tensioned framing system that was pioneered by the engineer Buckminster Fuller in his geodesic domes, such as the Climatron in St Louis. Inside the crystalline pyramid, 21 metres (70 feet) high and clad in polished laminated glass, the visitor descends to a marble-lined hall, to be directed to the various galleries of the Louvre. A diamond in the crown of Paris it is also, some maintain, François Mitterrand's answer to Georges Pompidou.

Dozens of other major museums have been built in the 1980s, still more are on the drawing board or in process of construction. Just a few one could mention are Hans Hollein's State Museum at Mönchengladbach or the same architect's Museum of Modern Art at Frankfurt; Arata Isozaki's Los Angeles Museum of Contemporary Art and the Pavilion for Japanese Art in the same city designed by the late Bruce Goff and completed by Bart Prince; Renzo Piano's museum to house the collection of Domenique de Menil at Houston; and the Museum of Science and Industry at La Villette by the English architects Michael Dowd and Alan Stanton. An English architect was also responsible for what is probably the best-known and most-visited of the modern museums, the New State Gallery at Stuttgart designed by James Stirling, Michael Wilford and Associates. The winning scheme in a limited competition, it was opened in 1984.

Stirling's gallery is a large and complex composition, which also includes a chamber theatre, library and administration block, masterfully deployed on a hillslope above a multi-lane highway. Visitors emerging from the highway underpass have a choice of a ramp or stairs, edged with shocking pink hand-rails, to guide them to the main concourse where a curved, green-glazed hall gives access to the galleries. Two pedestrian routes divide the complex, one leading from the lower to the upper levels by way of a sculpture court rotunda, ramped on the inside, the other leading internally by way of galleries. 'Today we can look back and regard the whole of architectural history as our background', James Stirling has observed, and he makes many allusions in his building from an Egyptian column to a half-buried portico, to incomplete stonework. It is, he says, a 'collage of old and new elements, Egyptian-like cornices, Romanesque windows, Constructivist canopies', many engaged in 'conversations'. Ingenious, witty, jokey in turns, Stirling's building has caught the breath, the imagination and the admiration of public and profession alike: a million people visited it within the first seven months, and most appear to have come to see the building as much as its contents. Some of its qualities are redrawn on modest scale at the Clore Gallery to house the Turners at London's Tate Gallery, though that building has been a disappointment to some observers.

Museums are public buildings, they are often well funded, frequently on prestigious and attractive sites, and both clients and architects seek to match the quality of the contents with the quality of their designs. The function of museums, however, can be – and is – called into question: what separates the modern museum from the former dilettante collector's 'cabinets of curiosities'; why *do* we collect the objects of the past and of other cultures, what purpose do they serve? Is their incarceration in museums an extension of our greed and lust for property? Whatever the answers to such questions may be, there is little sign of the boom in gallery-building diminishing. For our purposes they serve to illustrate the diversity of solutions to similar problems, the creativity of many architects and the pluralism which exists in design opportunities now that the tight bonds of a restrictive and puritanical modernism have been loosened. In so far as the labels invented for the dialogues of architects and critics have any real meaning, most of the 'isms' of contemporary architecture can be found in museum design: post modernism, free-style classicism, neo-vernacularism, even (in Gehry's Aerospace Museum) deconstructivism.

Museums are only one of a great many building types that constitute the built environment, as any local survey will rapidly confirm. But they are public buildings, to which access is comparatively easy, and they are almost invariably designed – or at least, adapted – by architects. But many another type might do as well; the point is, that in order to develop and test our criteria for contemporary architecture we need to have sufficient examples to make a comparison. By doing so we can begin to make a basis for architectural judgement that is not founded on prejudice, making an end to that tired philistine cliché, 'I don't know anything about architecture, but I do know what I like.'

Considering buildings as elements in the landscape, or in the cityscape, can result in regarding them as sculptural objects. Sometimes they may contribute to their context in the way in which a sculpture does, as a form in the round which arrests and holds our attention, which creates and moulds space. Buildings, by virtue of their size and numbers, also have to relate to the sites, very often the streets, in which they are situated. Some may be singular, the focus of route, an accent or a marker of an axis in the city. But others serve by being a part of the urban backdrop, not distinguished by their singularity but enjoyed as a part of a whole composition – like a house in a Georgian square. So the criteria that we may use for a museum are not necessarily those that we should use for another type of building.

Unlike a sculpture, or a backdrop for that matter, a building has to be experienced both inside and out. How a building 'looks' isn't enough; we cannot evaluate it on external appearances alone. We have to appreciate its spaces and volumes, its scale and proportions, its structure and its details. We have to consider how well it meets the demands placed upon it, how it creates an environment that suits its users, and how well it meets the functions for which it was designed. Architectural design is a complex activity, part art, part science, part social service; a building has to be assessed in terms that relate to the complexity of its design, production and use.

CHAPTER 11

The shrinking world

In the summer of 1987 what promised to be a major architectural event took place in the English seaside town of Brighton. After some fifteen years the International Union of Architects chose to hold its World Congress in Britain. July was also the time scheduled for the annual conference of the Royal Institute of British Architects, and as both organizers and hosts the RIBA decided to hold a joint UIA/RIBA Congress. On past experience as many as 5,000 architects from every part of the world, and virtually every country, were expected, as well as a substantial representation from Britain's large professional and student architectural bodies. The subject was a challenging one: 'Shelter and Cities – Building Tomorrow's World', very appropriate for what was declared by the United Nations as the International Year of Shelter for the Homeless.

There was something obscene about the high rates being charged for the best hotel rooms and for some of the excursions where delegates were to be extravagantly wined and dined: one ticket alone could feed many a Third World family for a year; a hotel room could pay for the building of a house in India or Indonesia. Perhaps it was all justified to ensure that the World Congress was fully attended. If so, it failed; by the opening of the conference a bare 700 delegates had registered. Trips were cancelled, whole conference halls closed, and events merged to ensure reasonable audiences, but at the end of the Congress both the RIBA and the UIA were in the red, and Rod Hackney, who had successfully campaigned to be president of both organizations, had a considerable headache to mark the occasion.

For those who attended there were many wise words and a worthy joint declaration. They were assured that the days of the prima donna architect were over – and showed their disagreement by flocking to the talks given by Richard Rogers and Remi Pietila. For the truth of the matter is that very few architects are sincerely interested in the problems of housing the world's homeless. Cities are of interest, if they mean mirror-glass-clad office blocks, foreign embassies, museums and other large and prestigious buildings. They are of little appeal if they imply the shelter of millions of the urban poor, and especially when the solutions may require the loss of personal fame as an architect. Not that architects are alone in this respect; anthropologists are far more attracted to doing their field work with remote and 'uncontacted' tribes than with the residents of squatter settlements, and resistant to using their skills in any applied way to advise on the improvement of conditions.

The problem of response to the world housing crisis goes far deeper than the failure of the Congress, as the whimper from the International Year of Shelter for the Homeless indicates. It may have been a modest success in various parts of the world but overall it was a failure. For one thing it should have been a decade, and not merely a year, as the campaign to provide water had been. For another, it failed to arouse the consciences or the sympathies of the affluent West sufficiently to be effective. As the major charitable organizations learned years ago, the ordinary member of the public can identify with the image of a single suffering child more readily than he or she can with the scale of a national disaster. But, as the response to the television reports on famine in Ethiopia confirmed, it is possible to stir the hearts and plumb the pockets of the privileged if they can visualize the tragic consequences of total deprivation. It seems that the lack of housing, or the squalid conditions of the urban slums in Third World cities, do not have the same emotional impact.

Nevertheless, the dimensions of homelessness and sub-standard housing throughout the world are immense, the numbers of people subsisting in frightful conditions without water, electricity, or sanitation virtually unimaginable. It was these issues that the UIA/RIBA World Congress attempted to address – though it would be illuminating to know how many people, if any, were decently housed as a direct result of its deliberations. At least 100 million people have no shelter over their heads of any kind, while the numbers of those who live in the poorest of rough shelters built from the discarded materials of the better-off run into hundreds of millions. These are disturbingly generalized figures, for the fact is no one knows exactly how many people are living in these circumstances.

One obstruction to understanding the problems of housing is the lack of any yardsticks by which conditions can be measured. The poorest housing in Britain, or in much of the United States, is better built and better serviced than most housing in the developing world – though the 'dosser' asleep in cardboard boxes on the Thames Embankment, or the 'bag-lady' asleep over a grating exhaling warm air from a New York restaurant kitchen, are as homeless as their counterparts in any country. Southern Blacks and 'poor Whites' in rural Arkansas or Alabama still live in two-room shacks of a kind that has hardly changed since the Civil War. Yet even these sagging dwellings, shamefully poor by comparison with the comfortable suburbs of many American cities, offer a level of accommodation to which untold millions will never be able to aspire. Admittedly, this is no comfort to those who are trying to raise a large family in a house lined with tar-paper, plagued with roaches, and serviced with an outside 'john'.

Obviously, there are numerous differences between the homeless bag-lady in New York and the black family in Arkansas; one difference is that while the former has probably gone to the city in search of work, the other, though poor, has stayed put in a rural environment. And though we could enumerate many others, this point is worth making because it underlines the reasons for the kinds of homelessness that are to be found in many countries. The city is a magnet for those who are out of work, as the rural areas can no longer support the large populations that they once could. Mechanization has made what was once labour-intensive farming now practicable with a tenth of the manpower. The 'green revolution', with new, high yield cereal strains, air-sprayed pesticides and chemical fertilizers, has made land more productive, even overproductive. Large landowners have profited from this. In the Third World they have also profited from Western pressure to produce cash crops such as tobacco rather than subsistence crops which might feed the local people. Together, these and other factors combine to force young people, and often whole families, off the land.

As rural regions become depleted or are recklessly exploited for short-term gain, tens of thousands of people move every week to the cities. There they may not be able to obtain regular work, but there may be *some* way of earning a living. It may be by recycling waste materials, or washing the clothes of the middle-class, or selling trinkets – and sisters – in the street. Small boys guard parked cars for a fee in Nairobi, women sell cakes of animal dung for fuel in Calcutta: where a niche in the city structure can be found, it is filled. Urban migrants exploit what has been rather cosily termed the economy of the 'informal sector', in their street-wise determination to survive.

The same necessary opportunism provides the drive behind the building of their shelters. Every kind of scrap and discarded material is pressed into service: industrial waste, bicycle tyres, packing cases, kerosene cans and anything else that might make a frame, a roof or wall covering, or might hold others in position. In the shadow of fashionable high-rise apartments in Bombay, a grey-brown undulating mass of rag-covered shacks smothers almost every available inch of ground on undeveloped lots, except for the maze of narrow footpaths, ankle deep in detritus, mud and excrement which threads between them. Alongside the railroads the unused ground is covered with shacks perched precariously above the tracks. As in most similar settlements, the squatters may fight running battles with the authorities, and may lose their shacks when the sites are to be developed. Yet in no time they will reappear elsewhere, tenaciously clinging to an alley, a plot of marshy ground, a stretch of beach, as they try to secure a stake in the city.

A similar story can be told about 'squatter settlements' in literally scores of cities across the world. The term is one which is widely used to describe collectively the unauthorized expansion of the urban areas. Most such settlements are built by migrants from rural areas, and this is sometimes reflected in the kinds of houses that are built and the village-style organization of the communities; this can be seen in the *kampungs* of Sumatra, for example, where even the name is one which is traditionally applied to villages. But the settlements on the peripheries of cities are also built by those for whom the pressures of inner city living become intolerable: many of the inhabitants of the *barriadas* of Lima, Peru, occupied barren lands outside the city, rather than suffer confinement within it. *Kampungs* and *barriadas* are on very dissimilar sites and they do not even look the same; the materials of which they are built are different (woven mats over frames in the *kampungs*, adobe earth blocks in Peru), but they are also socially dissimilar. They even grow differently, the *barriada* sites being invaded by large numbers of people virtually spontaneously and often on a fete day when the police are fully occupied elsewhere. In Casablanca, Morocco (and many other places) the settlements are called *bidonvilles* because the houses are built of *bidons*, or cut and flattened oil drums, which produce large metal sheets suitable for cladding walls. Kerosene and other types of can are used for the same purposes elsewhere. The *favelas* of Brazil, the *ranchos* of Venezuela, the *canicos* of Mozambique, the *gecekondus* of Turkey and the parallel urban settlements of many other countries have a number of elements in common, but many that are special to each one.

Generally, squatter settlements are technically illegal, or at any rate, unauthorized. Sometimes the settlers may own the land they occupy, but the building process itself is not legal; in other cases, the fact that houses are built is condoned, but there is no legality in the occupation of the land. Land is an important issue, because it is only with security of tenure that people can feel confident enough to make their makeshift homes more permanent. Yet, the land that is occupied is sometimes owned by an absentee landlord; sometimes, as in the case of the Turkish *gecekondus*, it is owned by the government. And there are cases in locations as far apart as Ecuador and Papua New Guinea where land is unavailable and unoccupiable, and so rickety raised plank-walks lead to houses built on stilts over the sea. Many of the locations are vulnerable in one respect or another: subject to flooding, landslides, or subsidence. But if the sites are often marginal, the role that the urban immigrants play in the city is not. Many squatters have regular jobs and stable relationships; what they lack is housing. Others may be desperately poor, but their willingness to do the work that others will not do means that the city frequently depends on them. From the reclining seats in their air-conditioned coaches many tourists see the *barracas*, the packing-case hovels of the poor, and join in the chorus of objections to the 'unsightly' dwellings. And a number of governments, anxious to attract tourists, remove those that are near the highways or the airport. But there are problems in clearing the slums; no government likes to be seen taking such action, it is not a politically wise move, as many of the settlers who live in them are well aware. They, after all, are voters, even if they do not pay taxes. The occupants of the settlements help to make the city function and total demolition of their homes is likely to be counter-productive, even if it were possible.

What the squatters generally require is recognition, and the legalizing of their settlements. But local governments are seldom enthusiastic about 'adopting' illegal settlements and committing themselves to the considerable additional expense of supplying main services to them. This was the dilemma that faced the authorities in Ankara, though they were among the very first to legislate in favour of the squatters. In a sense they had to; the *gecekondus* constitute three-quarters of the entire city. They exchanged the provision of some services – like schools – for the building of roads by the squatters themselves, and by 'trading' this way they supported the settlements at less cost. But the *gecekondus* have a higher level of housing based on traditional types than is usual, the residents retaining close ties with their original villages.

So there is a range of quality from the almost unimaginable deprivation of the *bustees* of Calcutta to the solid and serviced houses of Ankara or Istanbul. Likewise there is a range of economic and political contexts within which the settlements are built. There is little doubt that exploitation of the poor by privileged minorities frequently lies behind the conditions that force people to leave the rural areas for the city, and those that they find when seeking some kind of work within the city. Some would argue that any attempt to alleviate the discomfort within the squatter settlements only serves to shore up the iniquities of the systems that generate them in the first place. Others would maintain that every family has the right to move to, and work in the city if it wishes, and that the determination to find a site and build a house displays a courage and initiative that deserves to be supported. Realistically, people will move to the cities whatever the economic and political context, unless the regime is so repressive as to forbid it, or so controlled as to direct labour only where the state permits it.

If, then, the reality of the modern world is that the cities will continue to expand, what will be their ultimate scale? Unfortunately, the growth of cities is more accurately perceived in retrospect than in anticipation; estimates as to the population of Mexico City by the end of the century range from twenty millions to over twice that figure. Part of the uncertainty relates back to what the city acknowledges to be within its official limits: are the 'illegal' settlements a part of the city, or not? Whatever the size of the world's cities in the twenty-first century, there is no doubt that housing problems of almost unthinkable proportions lie ahead. Who is to be responsible for them? To what extent can the present infrastructures of Third World cities, already overburdened, be made to cope with these numbers? And what part can architects play in ensuring that people, hundreds of millions of them, can be decently housed with dignity and reasonable expectations of comfort?

These, of course, were the kinds of question that the UIA/RIBA World Congress intended to confront. Not that there is a total lack of architects and planners concerned with the problem;

a number have followed the leads given in the 1960s by Charles Abrams, John F. C. Turner and Aprodicio A. Laquian, among others. Even so, relative to the scale of urban growth they are still far too few. There are many aspects to the problems, but a distinction can be made between those presented by the existing settlements, and those that will be posed by future expansion in the cities. Some of these are created by the sheer costs involved in supplying such basic services as mains water, or sewerage disposal, let alone those generated by improving the building stock. Someone has to pay and somehow the money has to be recovered. Many countries have discovered that loans from the World Bank carry many conditions, that do not necessarily work to the advantage of the settlers; others have discovered that the cost of recovering their own loans to squatters may be greater than the expected returns.

One system that has been employed is 'Settlement Upgrading', which concentrates more on the improvement of the infrastructure than of the houses. So roads, water supplies, drainage trenches and electricity power lines are priorities. Sanitation is a major issue but water-borne disposal is by no means always practicable, and public latrines and solid waste disposal systems may be more feasible. Improvements may cause residents to give up space, but residents in upgraded *kampungs* in Surabaya, Java began to improve pathways on their own initiative and even to install street lighting. Squatter communities are understandably anxious about the fate of their settlements when government intervention is imminent, and it is evident that public participation in the planning process makes for a higher rate of success.

Planning is largely concerned with urban structure, as this may be forecast and, with a measure of control, organized in the future. Inevitably the degree of control is also a measure of the limitation on individual freedom which is permitted in taking decisions on the location of intended buildings, the materials that may be used, the space provision that is acceptable, and so on. If we think of planning procedures of Britain for a moment, we know that planning offices have quite precise rules on the building lines, roof heights, living densities, ceiling heights, even window sizes that are permissible. Grants to improve old buildings are often given only on the condition that proposed modifications meet these requirements. For more than a decade public funded housing was required to meet 'Parker Morris' standards, so called after Sir Parker Morris, the chairman of the committee which produced the report *Homes for Today and*

Tomorrow in 1961. There are many who feel that these standards should never have been withdrawn.

Planning regulations of this kind were drawn up specifically for application in Britain, and like any planning legislation they are assumed to be for the general good. In fact, though, they often favour the moderately well-off middle classes, and have been seen as repressive measures designed to protect the interests of one sector of the community at the expense of others. Be that as it may, it is hard to see such planning standards being applicable to Third World cities of the kind we have been discussing. But in fact this happens; in Kenya, Parker Morris standards were still being applied to new housing in the 1970s, and 'permanent' materials are still required for new developments. This means brick or concrete and not 'temporary' materials like timber and mud, even though these have proven durability. The argument for insisting upon such standards is partly one of pride: why should housing in the developing countries be of a 'poorer' standard than that in the West? Consequently, only the rich can afford the approved materials, and government provision of houses to the desired standard is minimal, expensive and incapable of meeting the insatiable demand of the new migrants. So the squatter settlements continue to grow.

However, there has been a movement, which started in Peru in the 1960s and has slowly gained acceptance, which considers planning measures to be appropriate to the growth of new settlements. What is more, settlers are allocated sites on which to build and basic facilities are brought to them. These 'Sites and Services' schemes require agreements with the intending occupants, who may have to give guarantees that they will complete building within a specified time, will not sell or lease off part of their assigned plots, will meet the schedule of repayments of loans, or other limitations. But they are assured of the security of their sites and may be supplied with water, electricity, drainage, probably garbage disposal, even public transport. Just who is eligible for the sites presents problems, for a regular income, length of time on the waiting list, size and age of family and other factors may be taken into account. So the poorest and newest arrivals may not necessarily benefit. But such Sites and Services schemes do bring housing in reach of many needy families. Sometimes a 'core' of a basic water supply, drainage and sanitation may be supplied, to which the framework of a house can be added; a method which has been used with success in Nairobi. Only one or two countries, like Tanzania, have developed such projects as the basis of their official housing policy.

In all these schemes the motivation of the new settlers to build is being capitalized upon. But in most instances the kind of housing they have experienced is either that of their rural villages, or the shanties of the city that they have inhabited on arrival. The range of possibilities open to them tends to be limited. Traditional buildings are rarely suitable in the city – the materials may not be available and often such buildings occupy too much space. Moreover, migrants have left the village anyway, and though they like to maintain contact with their rural origins they have chosen to be part of the city and want to build in an urban way.

The self-build impulse

As we have noted already, it is the desire on the part of families to build their own dwellings that makes Sites and Services schemes possible. In fact, mass housing solutions based on large-scale housing projects and rows of multi-storey blocks have been unsuccessful because the occupiers felt no sense of identification with the projects, and had no part to play in their construction. In Britain this may seem rather difficult to appreciate, because we have been accustomed to having housing built to the designs of specialists by local authorities or speculative builders. Few people have much say in the house in which they live, and although there have been sporadic attempts at 'self-build', as it is rather curiously termed, it is hardly a widely accepted means of obtaining a home. One or two architects, like the late Walter Segal, have seen the advantages of producing designs which provide a good standard of housing with the kinds of skills that any handyman may have. But not many.

Usually, vernacular architecture was 'self-built' or at any rate, community-built, but this tradition has long disappeared in Britain. In the early decades of this century, however, you could still buy a seaside plot at Canvey Island, Jaywick Sands or Shoreham Beach for as little as £20. Prefabricated light-weight houses could be bought cheaply and delivered to the site, or building materials could be brought in the family Ford Popular. Or, if you chose, you could recycle a horse-drawn pantechnicon or a railway carriage and adapt it to make a weekend holiday home. Between the wars thousands of London families obtained a plot and a house for an outlay of £50. The most visible and least developed of these 'plotlands' was at

Peacehaven, near Brighton, and it became a symbol of the spoliation of the coast by 'uncontrolled' development, the kind that the Town and Country Planning Act of 1947 was designed to curtail. Today, the kind of initiative that the building of the plotlands houses represents is reduced to pigeon lofts and allotment sheds.

Planning regulations are a little less restrictive in a number of European countries and a variety of well-cared-for weekend houses stand in garden plots in Copenhagen, and along the railroad verges in West Berlin. In many of the American states it is still possible, if you can obtain a site, to build your own log cabin, and there are training courses devoted to this form of vernacular romanticism. More remarkable are the structures and houses built by American eccentrics and individualists, like the celebrated decorated armatures, the 'towers' of Simon Rodia in Watts, Los Angeles. Over a period of thirty years from 1921 this illiterate Italian immigrant achieved his ambition to 'do something big'. Other examples include the five-storeyed timber ziggurat-house of Clarence Schmidt on Ohayo Mountain, Vermont; the house built of rolled newspapers at Pigeon Cove, Massachusetts by Elis Stenman; David Brown's Glass House made of embalming fluid bottles at Duncan, British Columbia; or the 'Log Cabin' and Garden of Eden built of limestone and concrete by S. P. Dinsmond at Lucas, Kansas. They are regarded as the work of American naives, primitives, or folk builders but in the 1960s and '70s, when communes and drop-out communities released unexpected gifts, many original 'wood-butcher's' houses were built by families with little or no previous experience. In Sauselito, California they extended on jetties and rafts into San Francisco Bay, tolerated for years as a tourist curiosity, before pressure was brought to bear to remove them – and architect-designed fashionable versions were built in their stead.

Then there were the non-architects who designed their own houses (like Carl Jung, Wittgenstein, Mark Twain, Jack London), and artists who designed fantastic buildings and romantic dream palaces (like Edward James, Niki Saint Phalle and Hundertwasser). Of course, not everyone has such reserves of creativity, or the motivation to build their own dwellings; the point is, that given the resources and the opportunity, many have. The cultural contexts in which these examples have occurred are ones where a variety of choices is available. In the contexts of developing countries the 'models' on which new builders could base their new homes are far fewer, and architects could do an invaluable service by extending their range of choice. Most architects' solutions to the need for low-cost housing have been rows of replicated units of numbing monotony, reflecting neither social patterns nor individual aspirations. It is clear that in the future a close partnership between the new residents of the urban settlements and architect–planners will be essential.

Unfortunately, very few architects have risen to the challenge so far. Those that have attempted to respond to the occasional competitions on the subject have designed housing that was impractical or too expensive to be of help to the poor. Yet their experience and skills would be invaluable in advising on greater variety of forms and structures, improved building methods and materials, effective passive climate modification and functional, but socially appropriate, internal spatial organization. Is it too much to ask that the urban settlements of the twenty-first century might be more humane, even beautiful? It seems that there is much for the architect with a concern for society to contribute to housing the expanding populations of the world's cities.

CHAPTER 12

Invitation to architecture

THE blessing and the curse of architecture is that we are all involved in its production, maintenance and appreciation. According to the late Sir Nikolaus Pevsner: "A bicycle shed is a building; Lincoln Cathedral is a piece of architecture." In the preceding pages, we hope to have shown, among other things, that the decision as to when bicycle sheds are architecture and when they are not is as open to debate as whether chocolate chip cookies significantly contribute to the sum of humankind's culinary achievements. Despite all the erudition that may be exercised in the furtherance of a point of view in this debate, a very few bicycle shed fanciers can reasonably claim the point proven by the weight of their collective judgement.

If we have any interest in architecture at all, then few would argue that it can but be enhanced by giving time to broadening our experience as the basis for critical appreciation. For some, this may mean simply consciously experiencing more buildings. In appreciation, as well as in design, there are those who feel that in the late twentieth century we are led to over-intellectualize what should properly be a more emotional and intuitive response to the world and its artefacts. Others will want deliberately to study the background to the production of certain forms of architecture. Yet again there will be those enthusiasts who wish to concentrate their attention on the development of architectural form in some particular locality or branch of the art.

An interest in architecture, like any interest in a particular aspect of human endeavour, may be driven by unconscious and conscious quests for many things, from simple pleasure or seeking after knowledge for its own sake, to more particular interests in architecture as a part of cultural, religious, social, technological, artistic or economic development.

Like any subject that has some involvement, however minor, in all aspects of human activity, its diversity of intention and achievement is, as we hope to have shown, highly controversial. Attitudes to the development of buildings are coloured and formed by concepts of history, philosophy and political economy, as well as those of art and technology.

Nevertheless, many observers still find it possible to admire buildings simply from the point of view of their appearance, or the way that they 'feel' as they walk around them. Equally, there are architects for whom the achievement of a timeless quality in a building remains far more important than its commissioning by the initial client or patron.

Buildings, like our human companions, are often much easier to get on with as acquaintances rather than as close colleagues and friends. Architectural commentaries are full of cases of internationally admired buildings that cause their everyday users inconvenience or even downright misery. In a field of endeavour that encourages prototypical solutions, it is inevitable that many good ideas should be marred by a range of conceptual or functional failures. It is inevitable also that some of these will be 'landmarks' in the development of style or technology, despite the failings which are perhaps only revealed by intimacy.

In most instances it is unlikely therefore that our views concerning architecture will be entirely balanced. It is not at all uncommon to hear phrases like: 'as a piece of sculpture I really like it, but as a building to use . . .'; or 'if it were a factory I'd think it was pretty good, but as a church . . .'; or again 'as an example of the style I think it's great, but in that setting . . .', and so on. Once we start to think about expressing any view about architecture we instinctively look for relationships between form and functioning, image and content. Just as inevitably, we will quickly come to views of these relationships which conflict with those of our neighbour, the local bureaucracy, the developer or the architect.

But because we all use buildings, because, in however small a way, we contribute to the need for them, and provide resources for their construction and upkeep, we all have a right to voice a view about them. We may choose to place the *artistic intentions* of the architect of our school low down in the list of our concerns with a building that freezes us in winter and bakes us in the summer sun. On the other hand, we may be happy to don extra layers of clothing when we attend a service in our medieval church and delight in its spatial qualities, constructional solidity and rich detail.

It is probably true that we are generally less forgiving of any failings in new buildings than we are of those in older ones. Certainly, since the notion of 'progress' became current in our societies, we have reasonably expected the new at least to perform functionally better than the old. We have seen in our discussion of 'modernism' that this fundamental belief can be shaken, yet for many people the attraction of 'neo-vernacular' and 'postmodern classicism' is the very promise that they might combine the benefits of both old and new.

The combination of the benefits of the best of the old with the best of the new is what many people would like to see in their everyday environment. It sounds easy doesn't it? Yet in reality, of course, this admirable intention not only holds a different meaning for almost every individual, but automatically leads us into the battleground of the competing interests who engage in the processes of physical change in our villages, towns and cities. Let's not deceive ourselves that these 'interests' are all multi-national companies or rapacious commercial developers; they are just as much you or I wishing to put a new extension on the side of our house, or the small farmer who wants to pull down a tumbledown 300-year-old barn to make way for a new tractor shed.

Since we began to lose faith again in the benefits of abstract modernism at the end of the 1960s, the protection and conservation of old buildings has been a common rallying point for those concerned with the quality of our built environment. Once again, after an interruption of almost half a century, the architecture of the past has become a reference for architects of the present, as well as the focus for a nostalgic reaction to the products of modernism. Our appreciation of the continuum of accretive development in our historic settlements, and the quality and value of fine old buildings, places both modernism and postmodernism within their historical and cultural context, in a way that enables us to identify again comfortably with the built environment.

If we are to better guide the development of the buildings in our villages, towns and cities, we need to enter actively into the debate. We cannot expect that everyone will want to take an interest, but if we do, we need to 'stand and be counted'. The actions of community and other interest groups have in the past achieved remarkable successes in preventing the destruction of historic buildings, or the development of inappropriate new buildings. The planning systems of more and more countries provide the opportunity, and sometimes other resources, to enable groups and individuals with strong views to make their case and participate in the development decision-making process.

These interventions in what is normally the preserve of professionals, puts everyone on their mettle. The interest group may well be offered the opportunity to make a case, but the effectiveness with which this opportunity is exploited will depend on a great deal of study, argument, organization, presentation and persuasion. For their part, the professionals will often find themselves uncomfortably required to redefine their jargon in common speech, without losing the force of their expert arguments. This is entirely appropriate, if only because we do all experience buildings, and whilst we may need to learn some of the technicalities of problems that lead to building solutions, we may equally be happy to leave this to the professional, yet still require to know why we should accept solutions that are apparently less than ideal. Whilst some may cry that it is as senseless as crushing a flower with a mallet, it can be salutary to hear architects defend their art in the face of questioning from a barrister in a planning inquiry. The scene may be even more compelling when the questioner is herself a lay enthusiast rather than a lawyer or an architect.

Few would question the painter's need for mastery of technique. At the same time, few would expect to have full insight into the beauty and meaning of a picture without some study. More observers are likely to be interested in the messages that the artist wishes to transmit than the technical means he employs to communicate them. So it is likely to be with the altogether more public art of architecture. In the seventeenth and eighteenth centuries, when much of the architecture was produced in Europe that is currently so admired, patrons and admirers of the art were often as versed in the artistic values and rules as the architects themselves. In fact, of course, many patrons were involved in user participation in design. Today, we are all more or less patrons. If we use public and commercial buildings or pay taxes or own a few shares, we have a direct stake in the production of buildings to serve the needs of these interests.

But what of the artist? He has his concerns and his rights. As we have seen it is often claimed that architects have become increasingly detached from the realities of construction. Superficially this may be true, yet the truth of the argument does rather depend on how we regard the lineage of the architect. We may never know the detail of the artistic relationship between the master mason and the clerics in the production of Gothic cathedrals, but for all his knowledge, we can hardly regard Sir Christopher Wren as a muddy-booted builder.

And those neo-classicists of the seventeenth and eighteenth centuries were sometimes master builders, but most notably they were gentlemen of leisure, aided by master builders.

The nineteenth-century developments in technology and the failure of all but the best of architects to master the use of new materials and techniques, and the failure of Modern Movement architects in the twentieth century to achieve successful technical mastery of glass, steel and concrete in the smooth, flat-roofed forms of the international style, have both fuelled the argument that the architect is divorced from the realities of construction. Architects themselves show the highest admiration for buildings which they see as being highly 'resolved', that is, consistent in execution from the siting and overall concept, through to the smallest detail. Indeed buildings described by architects as being 'unresolved' in their detail commonly display an ignorance or disregard for the appropriate use of materials. We have seen also that the Arts and Crafts Movement in England, and the Deutscher Werkbund and the Bauhaus in Germany, all placed great emphasis on the architect's ability to design small scale artefacts as well as buildings.

The concern with the relationship between overall design 'concept' and the detail appropriately resolved in keeping with it – in other words, total design control and concept realization – has been with us since at least the eighteenth century 'Age of Reason'. Since that time architects have sought to test their new ideas in domestic buildings. The dialogue between the architect and the client/user in the design of the individual dwelling has been a persistent forum for the presentation, interrogation and development of new thematic ideas, often later extended and proselytized in less personal design contexts. Architects from Palladio to Philip Johnson have used private domestic commissions in this way. We have seen that some contemporary architects have similarly used the design of *chic* London eateries to try out design concepts in a restricted and sympathetic context before attempting a more general application.

In the development of a design approach, every architect will have a design agenda. The relationship of this agenda to the socio-economic context of development will vary. Most architects have a concern to develop their work through design experience, but they will have differing views concerning the lessons of practice and the relationship of these lessons to their own artistic development. We have seen that Niels Prak identifies a distinct difference of approach and concern between the 'artistic' and the 'practical' architect, and whilst this is certainly a simplification, it is a convenient and useful one. On the whole, most modern movement 'masters' are clearly 'artistic' in their approach rather than 'practical'. In the 'postmodern' world, there are a surprising number of major figures who have only turned from theoretical academic work to significant practice comparatively late in their careers. Those, like James Stirling or Philip Johnson who appear to have moved with comparative ease from a 'modern' to a 'postmodern' approach, are relatively uncommon.

Perhaps the purist inheritors of the modernist legacy are the 'hi-tech' architects. The form of their buildings is generated by a celebration of technology. Often this has led to a somewhat over-engineered appearance, as in Grimshaw's Oxford ice skating rink or the similar design for a sports centre in the Merseyside Borough of Knowsely. The 'honesty' of the Pompidou Centre in hanging its entrails on the outside has little to do with functional requirements and much more to do with the expression of a demonstrative faith in technology. This could be traced back to the Romans, but more reasonably starts with the exposed engineering solutions to large-span problems in the train sheds and exhibition buildings of the nineteenth century and may yet reach its apotheosis in the realization of Archigram's visions of a development future with more in common with the forms of space conquest than the cultural baggage of our past.

Whether or not they are demonstrably 'hi-tech', most modern architectural solutions incorporate an impressive array of modern technology. Neo-vernacular housing is often a precisely engineered, highly serviced product. Even the highly traditional forms used by the English neo-classicist Quinlan Terry for offices on the banks of the Thames are equipped with sophisticated artificial illumination and air-conditioning systems. We have seen that the special buildings of our times like museums and art galleries require complex environmental control systems to regulate lighting, heating, ventilation and humidity for the protection of the exhibits and the comfort of the visitor.

Increasingly, the architect is part of a well-qualified building production team. The role of the architect as leader of this team is constantly under review. Corporate clients, for whom buildings sometimes are simply a link in the investment/production chain, may opt for an expert client and project coordinator as team leader. In the development of other commercial buildings it is not uncommon for the cost controller or quantity surveyor to chair team meetings and ensure that all design and production inputs are rationally discussed in accordance with the client's priorities.

These developments are viewed with dismay by many, yet the truth is that in large and complex building projects seldom ever has one individual been able to exercise complete and effective control. Most patrons, be they corporate or individual, want major investments to be things of pride, and whilst in some cases the architect may no longer be nominally in control of the design or construction processes, her design contribution remains a major concern. The univalence of many major examples of architecture and urban design may be seen as a product of design for the many by an individual. By contrast the richness of larger historic buildings and urban centres and districts is in part the result of numerous hands at work in their design and construction.

But without doubt society gets the architects and the architecture it deserves. For while artistic elites may be happy to practise at the fringes in the furtherance of ideals which are truly esoteric in the eyes of the mass of the populace, the products of an age will be judged by the full surviving range of its building output. The range of buildings that make up this output will certainly reflect the diversity of our pluralistic society, but the evidence of this is likely to highlight the functional and artistic poverty of the mass of work at the core. It is to be hoped that the third quarter of the twentieth century will remain its architectural nadir, for there have been recently many hopeful signs.

As the once dominant influence of modernism finally fades, we are gradually acquiring new generations of architectural teachers for whom alternative design approaches were available during their own formative student years. In the bigger schools of architecture no one style prevails as the normative approach. The fruits of the wide-ranging debate of architectural education which took place in the 1960s have ripened. We know now that sociologists and educational psychologists do not have all the answers, but many of the lessons they do have to teach have become an accepted part of the education of the architect. The democracy of post-war Europe and the nature of the postmodern market economy have led to architects being required to explain their proposals rather than expecting a grateful world to accept them as the gifts of art.

At the same time, both practising town planners and planning schools now spend more effort on issues of design than zoning, both conditioned by the failures of past plans and controls and the pressures of current *laissez-faire* capitalism. Across the world there is an increasing demand for the *urban designer*, positively bridging between planning and design and, it is hoped, constructively mediating between commercial and community interests. The practice of urban design is underpinned by these notions, and is committed to a practical and artistic consideration of the urban context of the work: the district identities, linkages, morphology and built resources of redundant buildings.

In an unprecedented way architecture has quite recently become a subject of popular debate. Radio, television and the newspapers now all carry more articles on architectural matters. In Britain, Prince Charles, following in the footsteps of his ancestor the Prince Consort, Albert, continues to make the public invitation to architecture headline news, even whilst these words are being written, with a measured television presentation of his own view of the architectural failures of the recent past and hopes for the future. These views are presented by an informed layman, whose hobby might be said to be an appreciation of classical architecture and the preservation of our historic townscapes, whilst his social concerns include access for ordinary people to decent humane buildings for living and working, that fit pleasantly in their surroundings. The urbane and privileged Prince, despite all his modesty, can hardly be characterized as a 'Mole', in the terms of the essays comparing the 'Mole' and 'Corb' approaches to design (see chapter 9), yet he certainly sides with the Moles, and it is to be regretted that in their ripostes of his criticisms, the architectural establishment, like the student author mentioned before, appear to be cutting themselves off from the human race.

However, whilst some sections of the architectural establishment were wringing their hands at the Prince's judgements, we can scarcely ignore the fact that at the same time the president of the Royal Institute of British Architects was Dr Rod Hackney, a leading 'community architect'. From the early 1970s community architecture became the active concern not just of a few 'sixties generation' architects and their community clients, but also of governments across the world. The essence of the approach is that the architect becomes an 'enabler' putting the range of his skills at the disposal of client groups, who are then able to have *their* ideas and concerns translated into building.

In Britain such community projects have enabled public sector housing tenants from Glasgow to the London borough of Hackney to refurbish out-of-date housing as they wish, using public money. Elsewhere, other groups have built new housing and community buildings designed by themselves with the help of architects, as in Liverpool or in Telford and the London borough of Lewisham where 'ordinary people' not only designed their houses, but built them too. As we have previously discussed, in countries where rapid urbanization is taking place, similar initiatives are used to house those with no access to the housing products of government programmes or the private sector. Here sites are often provided with road access, water, electricity and other services, whilst groups of residents pool labour and skills to build traditional homes that are more successful than the Western system-built apartment blocks that so many countries bought in an attempt to stem massive housing demand. The success of such projects is inevitably variable, but overwhelmingly they achieve a far greater control over their domestic environment for the participants than they could otherwise achieve.

Architecture offers a truly rich and varied diversion, study or career. It has the almost unchallengeable advantage that, apart from our sojourns in the wilderness, it is always with us: buildings provide the stage or the backdrop for all our activities. As a student, practitioner, or enthusiast we can enjoy our interest all the day long at home, work or play and the journeys between. When we tire of the everyday, we can make special pilgrimages, which give us the experience not only of our goal and its architectural context, but the delights along the unaccustomed route that we take to reach it. We can learn about every aspect of human endeavour from the living archaeology of the buildings that house and have housed them. In addition to all of this, whatever our particular interest, we can act as a curator, defender and promoter of our environment and its architecture. There is an invitation in architecture for us all.

Further reading

The following titles have been selected for their relevance to the various parts of this book. Some are more technical than others, but in many aspects of the subject there are no readily obtainable general introductions. Most of these books are available in paperback, but some may only be obtainable from a library. There are alternatives, and we recommend that you ask for permission to browse in the library of your nearest architectural school.

PART I   ARCHITECTURE FOR ALL

Alex Clifton Taylor, *Buildings of Delight* (ed. D. Moriarty), Gollancz, 1986.
   A lively collection of essays by a man with a knowledgeable, infectious delight in the vernacular buildings of England.

David Harvey, *Social Justice and the City*, Edward Arnold, 1973.
   The first and most accessible of an impressive series of books by this author on the complex concerns of social justice in the production and use of the urban environment.

Kevin Lynch, *The Image of the City*, MIT Press, 1960.
   By far the most enduring and influential attempt to provide a means of explaining our perception of the form of cities, both existing and in design.

Spiro Kostoff, *A History of Architecture*, Oxford University Press, 1987.
   Though it emphasizes architecture in the West, this is a sound, well-illustrated work. All you need to know about history (?).

C. Norberg Schultz, *Intentions in Architecture*, MIT Press, 1965.
   A philosophical view by a Norwegian theorist who considers what we mean by architecture and environmental quality – not an easy read.

Patrick Nuttgens, *Understanding Modern Architecture*, Unwin Hyman, 1989.
   A clear and useful guide by a popular academic commentator.

FURTHER READING

Paul Oliver, *Dwellings: The House Across the World*, Phaidon, 1987.
A cross-cultural survey of the one kind of architecture that everybody experiences; it examines the factors that have shaped housing.

PART II   ARCHITECTURE AND ARCHITECTS

Reyner Banham, *Theory and Design in the First Machine Age*, Architectural Press, 1960.

> How twentieth-century architectural ideas developed in the period before the advent of the electronic age. Art, architecture and industrial design are related in this complex, lively work.

Tim and Charlotte Benton with Dennis Sharp, *Form and Function: An Architectural Source Book*, Open University Press, 1975.

> A useful source book, which gathers together a number of manifestos and tells us what the architects and critics of the Modern Movement *really* wrote.

Robert Gutman, *Architectural Practice: A Critical View*, Princeton University Press, 1988.

> An examination of recent changes in the architectural profession with particular reference to the United States, but dealing with issues of practice that concern all Western architects.

Peter Hall, *Cities of Tomorrow*, Basil Blackwell, 1989.

> A mature, wide-ranging account of the people, ideas and events that have influenced the shaping of the cities of the world this century. An excellent comparative critique for future developments.

Alan Holgate, *The Art in Structural Design*, Oxford University Press, 1986.

> Much of the progress of nineteenth- and twentieth-century architecture has relied on the design skill of the structural engineer; Alan Holgate argues for a better integration now of artistic considerations with the science of structural design.

Rob Krier, *Architectural Composition*, Academy Editions, 1988.

> Krier dedicates his book to 'students of architecture, patrons, politicians and speculators', and though often idiosyncratic, this is an accessible, rich and informative book.

Le Corbusier, *Towards a New Architecture*, Architectural Press, 1946.

> The seminal work that inspired a generation of modern architects. Le Corbusier's enthusiasm for airplanes, grain silos and industrial technology is still exciting to read.

Raymond Lifchez, *Rethinking Architecture: Design and Physically Disabled People*, University of California Press, 1987.

FURTHER READING

Much broader in scope than the sub-title suggests, this book raises fundamental questions about approaches to design.

Andrew Orton, *The Way We Build Now: Form, Scale and Technique*, Van Nostrand Reinhold, 1988.

Although it assumes some prior knowledge, this book provides an easy-to-digest technical explanation of a well-illustrated range of modern buildings.

Nikolaus Pevsner, *The Sources of Modern Architecture and Design*, Thames & Hudson, 1968.

Pevsner traces the origins of modernist and functionalist architecture in the design developments of the late Victorian era.

Niels Prak, *Architects: The Noted and The Ignored*, Wiley, 1984.

A lively book which employs a wide variety of sources to illustrate the design concerns of practice and the relationships between 'artistic' and 'practical' architects.

PART III   ARCHITECTURE FOR TODAY

Brent Brolin, *The Failure of Modern Architecture*, Studio Vista, 1976.

Brolin argues that 'modernism' failed at both the architectural and the social levels.

Peter Collins, *Changing Ideals in Modern Architecture 1750–1950*, Faber & Faber, 1965.

Drawing on material from historiography to literature and criticism, this remains a challenging account of the movements of architecture in the period.

Charles Jencks, *The Language of Post-Modern Architecture*, Academic Press, 1977.

An entertaining and sometimes infuriating survey of the diversity of architectural styles which emerged with the demise of modernism.

Alan MacDonald, *The Weller Way*, Faber & Faber, 1986.

A readable account of how one group of ordinary Liverpudlians organized and achieved their own new housing, tackling everything along the way from bureaucracy to design and management.

Nicholas Negroponte, *Soft Architecture Machines*, MIT, 1975.

A comparatively early book on computers and architecture which still raises some of the more interesting arguments.

Victor Papanek, *Design for the Real World*, Thames & Hudson, 1972.

A classic study of the needs of ordinary people in many parts of the world, and how designers might meet the challenge they pose.

FURTHER READING

John F. C. Turner, *Housing by People*, Pantheon, 1971.

A work by the influential theorist of community action as a means of dealing with the expanding housing problems.

Peter Wilsher and Rosemary Richter, *The Exploding Cities*, Andre Deutsch, 1975.

There are many specialist studies of squatter settlements of the poor; this general work surveys the growing urban problems of the 'Third World'.

Lance Knobel, *The Faber Guide to Twentieth Century Architecture of Britain and Northern Europe*, Faber & Faber, 1985.

A reliable guide to 300 buildings of this century to see on your travels.

HRH The Prince of Wales, *A Vision of Britain*, Doubleday, 1989, see also Max Hutchison, *Building the Future*, Faber & Faber, 1989, and Jonathon Glancey, *New British Architecture*, Thames & Hudson, 1989.

Prince Charles' vision and two alternative views are essential reading for the British devotee.

Index

Aalto, Alvar, 58
Abrahams, Charles, 149
acoustics, 89
advertisement, 82–3, 93
Aerospace Museum, Los Angeles, 140, 142
Africa, 27, 29, 42, 43
aesthetics, 5, 83, 87, 88, 89, 90, 108, 100–11, 137, 139
Ahrends, Burton and Koralek (ABK) 1, 19, 133
air conditioning, 112
Albers, Josef, 68
Alberti, Leon Battista, 81, 85, 86, 107
Albi Cathedral, France, 86
Alexander, Christopher, 81, 131
anthropologists, 31, 144
Appeldoorn, Holland, 116
archaeology, 30, 162
Archigram, 138, 159
architect's brief, 57, 94–6, 97, 98
Architect's Co-Partnership, 18
Architect's Registration Council of the United Kingdom (ARCUK), 66, 73
Architectural Association School of Architecture, 67
architectural education, 6, 57, 63–77, 98, 160
architectural history, 37–46
architectural practice, 91–104
Arendt, Hannah, 130
art and artists, 68, 81, 82, 122–3
art galleries, 133–4, 138, 139, 140, 141, 159
Art Nouveau, 121
Arts and Crafts Movement, 123, 158
Arup, Sir Ove, 102, 133
Ashmolean Museum, Oxford, 20
Asian architecture, 40, 41, 42
Asplund, Gunnar, 129
autonomous house, 129
avant-garde, 81, 82, 126, 127
Avery Associates, 135
axonometric projection, 7, 70
Azay-le-Ridaud, France, 102, 133

Baillie-Scott M. H., 54
Baines, Sir George Grenfell, 102
Baker, Sir Herbert, 17
Banham, Reyner, 18, 82
Barabudur, Java, 42
Barlow, W. H., 110
Baroque style, 80
barriadas, 146
Barry, Sir Charles, 112
Bartlett School of Architecture, 67
basic design, 68
Bauhaus, 68, 71–2, 112, 158
Beaulieu, 11
Beauvais Cathedral, France, 39, 107
Beaux-Arts, Ecole des, 67, 72
Behrens, Peter, 111–12, 113
Berlage, H. P., 120
Berlin, 46, 53, 56, 58, 59, 92, 111, 152
Bernal, Professor, C., 107
Bernini, Gianlorenzo, 87
Bibliothèque Nationale, Paris, 120
Birmingham, England, 56
Bo, Jorgen and Wohlert, Vilhelm, 135
Bodleian Library, Oxford, 16
Bofill, Ricardo, 131
Bognar, Botond, 130
Bombay, 146
Box, W. R., 95
Bramante, Donato, 85
bricks, 18, 19, 23, 24, 29, 30, 109, 114
Broadacre City, 123
Brunelleschi, Filippo, 87
builders, 6, 14
building failure, 2, 106–7, 115
building regulations, 64, 65, 107
building standards, 107
building technology, 108, 109, 110, 111, 112
bungalows, 32, 35
Burnham, D. H. and Root, J. W., 121
Burrell Gallery, Glasgow, 139
Burton, Richard, 133
Butterfield, William, 18
Byker, Newcastle upon Tyne, 116
Byzantine style, 3

167

INDEX

cathedrals, 39, 78–9, 80, 106–7, 133–4
Centraal Beheer offices, Holland, 96
Centre Point, London, 85
Chambord, France, 11
chapels, 14
Charles, HRH Prince of Wales, 1–2, 4, 133, 161
Chartres Cathedral, France, 86
chateaux, 11, 16
Chichen Itza, Yucatan, Mexico, 41
China, 42, 43
Christ Church College, Oxford, 14, 15
churches, 15, 80, 89, 106
Churchill, Sir Winston, 48
'Cité Industrielle', 123
'Città Nuova', 123
city, 6, 12–13, 33–4, 49–50, 53–6, 59, 72, 79, 92, 123–4, 127, 128, 130, 132, 143–4, 145–8, 150
city density, 34
Classicism, 20, 40, 45, 46, 67, 79, 119, 133, 140, 142
client, 6, 19, 48, 91, 92, 93, 94, 95, 96, 97, 98, 100, 101, 102, 103, 104, 141, 158, 159, 160, 161
Climatron, St Louis, 140
Clore Gallery, London, 141
Cockerell, C. R., 20
colleges, 13–20, 52
colour, 87–8, 89
commission, 93, 94, 95
community action, 156–7
community architecture, 76, 81–2, 96, 116, 161
community needs, 3, 28, 29, 32, 49
competitions, 1, 16, 20, 93, 133, 153
computer aided design (CAD), 70, 103
computer programs, 66, 70
computer terminal, 69, 103
concrete, 112, 114, 121, 122, 123, 125, 127, 128, 134, 137, 150
condominia, 51
Congrès Internationaux d'Architecture Moderne (CIAM), 55, 124, 126
conservation, 3, 24, 51–2, 156
construction controls, 102–3
construction costs, 115
construction industry, 100–1, 103, 104, 114–15
construction methods, 30, 31, 64
Constructivists, 122
consultants, 100, 101, 102, 104
contractors, 99–100, 101, 102
contracts, 99, 101, 102
conversions, 3, 48–9, 64
Cook, Peter, 59
Copenhagen, 152

Cotswolds, England, 26, 29
Council for National Academic Awards (CNAA), 67
country cottage, 26–7, 29
craftsmen, 32, 39, 44, 80, 81, 109
criteria, 3, 6
critical appreciation, 154–5
criticism, 1–2, 35, 40, 84, 161
cruck-frame, 30
Crystal Palace, London, 82, 119, 120
Cubists, 123
Cullen, Gordon, 54

Deane, Sir T., 20
deconstructivism, 142
decoration, 87–8, 121
decorative arts, 121
Decorative Arts Museum, Frankfurt, 138–9
determinism, 48
developers, 2, 3, 50, 56, 98, 156
development control, 97
design, 1, 2, 5, 6, 32, 48, 50, 64–76 *passim*, 91–104 *passim*, 107, 110–16 *passim*, 121, 122, 123, 133, 134, 135, 136, 139, 140, 141, 158, 160, 161
design process, 98, 99
design solution, 98
design studio, 74, 75, 76
De Stijl, 123
Deutscher Werkbund, 111, 112, 126, 158
domes, 125, 140
Dowd, Michael and Stanton, Alan, 140
drawing, 7, 69–71, 103
Durand, J. N. L., 72
Dutert, C., 120

Egypt, 40, 42
Eiffel, Gustav, 121, 140
eighteenth century, 39, 45, 53, 119, 157, 158
Einstein Observatory, Potsdam, 125
Eisenmann, Peter, 59
elevation, 70
elevator, invention of, 122
Engels, Friedrich, 53
engineers, 71, 73, 89, 101, 102, 110, 111, 112, 113, 120, 121, 140
environmental control, 111, 112, 136, 139, 159
Erickson, Arthur, 135–6
Erlach, Fischer von, 43
Erskine, Ralph, 116
ethnocentrism, 41, 42
Europe, 56, 58, 63, 83
examinations, 64, 66, 67, 73, 92
Exchange, Amsterdam, 120
existenzminimum, 127

INDEX

Expressionism, 122–3, 125

factories, 22, 113, 122
Fagus Factory, Alfeld-an-der-Leine, 122
fan-vaulting, 14, 15, 16
Fiat works, Turin, 122
Fibonaci, 85
fire regulations, 114
Fletcher, Sir Banister, 37–8, 46
Florey Building, Oxford, 19
flying buttress, 38–9
form, building, 5, 6, 31, 40, 87, 120, 121
Formlehre, 68
Foster, Norman, 113, 131, 133
Foster Associates, 137
Frankfurt, 138–9, 140
Freyessinet, E., 121
Fuller, R. Buckminster, 140
function, 105, 106, 107–11, 113, 120, 122, 156
functional failure, 155, 161
functionalism, 6, 32, 121, 125

Galérie des Machines, Paris, 120
Garden City, 34, 54, 55, 114
Garnier, Tony, 123, 124
Gasson Associates, Barry, 139
gecekondus, 147–8
Gehry, Frank, 140, 142
genius loci (spirit of place), 50, 131
geodesic domes, 140
Georgian style, 84
Gibbons, Grinling, 11
Gibbs, James, 16
GLC Architect's Department, 137
Goetheanum, Dornach, Switzerland, 123
Goff, Bruce, 140
'Golden Section', 84–5
Gothic revival, 120
Gothic style, 14, 15, 20, 37–8, 39–40, 45, 78–9, 80, 85, 110
Grand Prix de Rome, 67
Grand Tour, La, 44, 45
Great Exhibition of 1851, London, 119
Greece, 26, 31, 40, 41, 44, 45
Greek Temples, 110
Green College, Oxford, 19
green revolution, 145
Greene, G. T., 112
Grimshaw, Nicholas, 25, 159
Gropius, Walter, 58, 68, 112, 122
Grosses Schauspielhaus, Berlin, 123
Guggenheim Museum, New York, 134
guilds, 109
Guimard, Hector, 121

Habitat, Montreal, 133
Hackney, Rod, 143, 161

Haghia Sophia, Istanbul, 41
half-timbering, 26, 35
Hancock building, Chicago, 132
Happold, Edward, 102
Haussmann, 53
Hawksmoor, Nicholas, 16
Hawley, Christine, 59
Hayward Gallery, London, 137
Heliodon, 66
Hellmuth, Obata and Kassabaum, 136
Hennebique, François, 112, 121
heritage, 3
Hertzberger, Hermann, 96, 116
high-rise buildings, 21, 36, 121–2, 124–5, 132
Hill House, Helensburgh, 123
Hilmer, Heinz, 46
historicism, 129
hi-tech, 25, 103–4, 113, 131, 138, 159
Holford, Sir William, 21
Hollein, Hans, 140
homelessness, 143, 144–5
Hongkong and Shanghai Bank, Hongkong, 133
Horta, Victor, 120
house purchase, 105
housing, 6, 23–5, 32–6, 50–1, 55, 56, 58, 59, 80–1, 82, 96, 97, 113–15, 127, 143–53, 161–2
housing, low cost, 153
housing density, 33, 97, 127
Howard, Ebenezer, 34, 54, 127
Hundertwasser, Friedensreich, 152
'Hvittrask', Helsinki, 123

India, 27–8, 42, 43, 55
Industrial Revolution, 33
infrastructure, 149
Interbau Exhibition, Berlin (1957), 58–9
interior decoration, 88
International Building Exhibition, Berlin (1987), 58–9
International style, 125, 158
International Union of Architects (UIA/IUA), 143, 144, 148
International Year of Shelter for the Homeless, 143, 144
iron, 20
Islamic architecture, 39
isometric projection, 70
Isozaki, Arata, 140
Italy, 41, 44
Itten, Johannes, 68

Jackson, Sir Thomas, 16–17
Jacobsen, Arne, 18
James, Edward, 152

169

INDEX

Japan, 42, 43, 133
Jencks, Charles, 129
Johnson, Philip, 132, 158, 159
Jones, Inigo, 44–5
Jugendstil, 121
Jung, Carl, 152

Kagawa and Sakakura Sekkei, 135
Kahn, Louis, 113, 125
kampungs, 146, 149
Kandinsky, Wassili, 68
Keble College, Oxford, 18–19
Kenya, 150
Kerr, George, 111
Khajuraho, India, 42
Klee, Paul, 68
Kostoff, Spiro, 43
Krier, Leon, 129
Kroll, Lucien, 116

Labrouste, Henri, 120
Lancaster, Sir Osbert, 113
land, 96–8, 147
land value, 97
landscape architects, 101
Laquian, Aprodicio A., 149
Le Corbusier (Charles Jeanneret), 31, 40, 54–8, 85, 88, 94, 102, 120, 123, 124, 125, 127, 129, 130, 133, 137
Le-Duc, Viollet, 40
legal protection, 92
legislation, 53, 107
Letchworth, Hertfordshire, 34, 54
liability, 65, 100
light, 87–9
lighting, 134, 136–7
Lincoln Cathedral, 38
Lincoln's Inn Fields, London, 90
Linz Cafe Project, Austria, 81
litigation, 100
Liverpool, 49, 114, 115
log cabin, 26, 31, 152
London, 34, 107, 110, 112
London County Council, 92
longhouse, 29
Loos, Adolf, 121
Louisiana Kunstmuseum, Copenhagen, 135, 140
Louvain, Belgium, 116
Louvre, Paris, 140
Lutyens, Sir Edwin, 54, 55, 124, 137
Lynch, Kevin, 50

Mackintosh, Charles Rennie, 123
Maison du Peuple, Brussels, 120
Mâle, Emile, 80
market research, 51

master builders, 80 81, 158
master masons, 14, 15, 16, 39, 44, 109, 157
materials, 2, 14, 20, 28, 29, 30, 64, 108–11, 112, 114, 115, 120, 125, 146, 150, 151
Matrix, 47
Medieval, 87, 119
Meier, Richard, 138
Melk monastery, Austria, 89
Melnikov, Kasimir, 122
Mendelsohn, Erich, 125
Merton College, Oxford, 14–15
Meso-America, 41–2
Metro, Paris, 121
Metroland, 34
Mewes and Davies, 112
Mexicali Housing Project, Mexico, 81–2
Meyer, Hannes, 68
Micklethwaite, J. T., 74
Mies van der Rohe, Ludwig, 68, 78, 112, 124, 125
migrants, 145, 146, 148, 151
Milton Keynes, 55, 56
Modernism, 6, 46, 119–31, 141, 156, 160
Modern Movement, 6, 41, 53, 54, 58, 72, 73, 79, 95, 102, 113, 119, 124, 126, 129
module system, 120, 124
Moholy-Nagy, Laszlo, 68
Montacute, 11
Monticello, N. Carolina, 11
Monument to the IIIrd International, 122
Morris, Sir Parker, 149–50
Morris, William, R., 22, 71, 81, 112, 119
Moser, Karl, 112
Moya, Hidalgo, 18
Musuem of Anthropology, Vancouver, 135–6
museums, 20, 133–6, 138, 139, 140–2, 159
Muslim expansion, 42
Muthesius, Hermann, 111, 112

National Air and Space Museum, Washington DC, 136, 140
National Gallery, London, 1, 133
National Museum of Art, Washington DC, 140
Nazca, Peru, 41
neo-classicism, 46, 83, 133
neo-Georgian, 113, 114
neo-rationalism, 129
neo-vernacular, 51, 113, 129, 142, 156, 159
Nervi, Luigi, 125
Neumann, Balthasar, 89
New Delhi, India, 124
New State Gallery, Stuttgart, 140–1
new towns, 20, 55, 56, 128
Niemeyer, Oscar, 58

170

INDEX

nineteenth century, 23, 34, 45, 53, 54, 115, 120, 158
node, 50
Notre Dame, Paris, 39
Notre Dame du Haut, Ronchamp, 133

Oakland Museum, California, 135, 140
office organization, 75, 98–9, 102
O'Gorman, Juan, 125
Olympic Stadium, Tokyo, 133
Open Air Museums, 30
Otis, E. G., 113
Oxford, 12–25, 45, 50, 113, 115

Pacioli, Luca, 84
package deals, 101
Palazzetto della Sport, Rome, 125
Palazzo Ducale, Venice, 88
Palladian style, 16
Palladio, Andrea, 45, 85, 158
Paris, 53, 121
Parker, Barry, 54
Parker Morris standards, 149–50
Paternoster Square, London, 2
Paxton, Sir Joseph, 82, 119
Pei, I. M., 140
Perret, Auguste, 112
perspective, 70, 86, 87, 89
perspective, aerial, 87
Pevsner, Sir Nikolaus, 82, 127, 154
phenomenologists, 130–1
physical laws, 108
Piano, Renzo, 138, 140
Pietila, Remi, 143
place, 5, 48–59
plan, 69, 70
planners, 6, 33, 34, 35, 56, 97, 148, 160
planning, 2, 6, 24, 25, 33, 34, 35, 50–1, 54, 123, 149–50, 156, 161
planning committees, 2, 3
planning regulations, 152
plotlands, 151–2
Poelzig, Hans, 122–3
Pompidou Centre, Paris, 84, 138, 159
population growth, 148, 153
postmodernism, 6, 46, 80, 83, 119, 129, 142, 156, 159, 160
post-war redevelopment, 24
Powell, Sir Philip, 18
power, political, 80
prairie houses, 123
Prak, Niels, 78, 93, 158–9
Prandtauer, Jacob, 89
prefabrication, 119, 125, 151
pre-industrial, 54
Prince, Bart, 140
privacy, 28

private domain, 53
problem-solving, 5–6, 56–7, 95
professional practice, 63, 64, 73, 74, 75
proportion, 46, 83–5, 86, 87, 142
Pruitt-Igoe Estate, Chicago, 125
psychologists, 160
psychology of architecture, 65
public domain, 53
Pugin, Augustus, 45
pupillage, 72, 74–5
pyramid, Louvre, Paris, 140

qualifications, 63, 64, 66, 67, 69, 71, 73, 74, 92
quantity surveyor, 71, 100, 101, 160

Radburn, New Jersey, 127
Radcliffe Camera, 16
railway stations, 82, 110, 120
recycling materials, 145–6
re-development, 24
regionalism, 32
Reid, David Boswell, 112
Reilly, Professor, 46
Reliance building, Chicago, 121
Renaissance, 14–15, 16, 17, 44, 81, 84, 87
Repton, Humphrey, 11–12
Richardson, H. H., 120
Richardson, Professor Albert, 46
Rietveld, Gerrit, 123
Roche, Kevin and Dinkeloo, John, 135
Rococo style, 88–9
Rodchenko, Alexander, 122
Rodia, Simon, 152
Roehampton Estate, London, 127
Rogers, Richard, 131, 138, 143
Romanesque style, 39
Rome, Italy, 41, 44, 45
Ronan Point, London, 125
Rossi, Aldo, 129
Royal Institute of British Architects (RIBA), 4, 64, 67, 73, 74, 143, 144, 148, 161
rural regions, 145, 146
Ruskin, John, 20, 45
Russia, 46, 122, 126

Saarinen, Eero, 123, 133, 135
Saarinen, Eliel, 123
Safdie, Moshie, 133
Sagebiel, 46
Sainsbury Centre, Norwich, 137
St Catherine's College, Oxford, 18
St John's College, Oxford, 18
St Mark's, Venice, 41, 88
St Pancras Station, London, 110
St Paul's Cathedral, London, 2, 11, 85
St Peter's, Rome, 87

INDEX

Saint-Phalle, Niki de, 152
sanitation, 33, 144, 145, 149, 150
Sant'Elia, Antonio, 123
Sattler, Christoph, 46
scale, 21, 84, 85–6, 89, 109, 125, 132, 136, 142
Schlemmer, Oscar, 68
Schmidt, Clarence, 152
schools of architecture, 6, 65–77
Schroeder House, Utrecht, 123
sciagraphy, 87
Scott, Geraldine, 135
Scott, Sir George Gilbert, 17, 20, 110
Scruton, Roger, 81
section, 70
Segal, Walter, 116, 151
self-build, 81–2, 129, 151
semi-detached house, 34–5
Serlio, Sebastiano, 44
services, basic, 147, 149
settlement, 28–9, 43, 53
settlement upgrading, 149
seventeenth century, 45, 157, 158
Sharp, Thomas, 24–5, 127
Shaw, Richard Norman, 54
Sheldonian Theatre, Oxford, 16
shelter, 43, 144–6
Siegal, Gwathmey, 134
site analysis, 96, 97, 98
site plan, 70, 96
sites, 5, 29, 96, 97, 98, 142, 146, 147, 150, 162
sites and services scheme, 150, 151
Sitte, Camillo, 54
sixteenth century, 44, 86
Smithson, Peter and Alison, 82
Soane, Sir John, 90
social requirements, 28–9
sociologists, 160
sociology, 130
South America, 41–2
space, 5, 31, 32, 49, 55, 59, 87, 89, 142
speculative housing, 151
Speer, Albert, 46
standards, 103
steel-frame, 112, 121, 125
Stein, Clarence, 127, 129
Steiner, Rudolf, 123
Stieglitz, Alfred, 39
Stirling, James, 19, 131, 140–1, 159
stone, 14, 18, 19, 20, 21, 26, 28, 29, 38
Strasbourg Cathedral, France, 39
structural failure, 106, 115
structural principles, 31, 64
suburbs, 5, 23–5, 32–6, 113
Sullivan, Louis, 120
surveying, 91–2
Sydney Opera House, 133
system-building, 127

Tafuri, Manfredo, 81
Tange, Kenzo, 133
Tatlin, Vladimir, 122
technical innovation, 5, 39, 114, 115–16, 120, 121–2
technology, 5, 6, 108
Teotihuacan, Central Mexico, 41
Terry, Quinlan, 83, 129, 159
Tessenow, Heinrich, 129
Third World, 143–51
Thompson, Michael, 129
Tiahuanaco, Peru, 41–2
Tiepolo, Giovanni Battista, 89
Tikal plaza, Peten, Mexico, 41
timber, 28, 38, 108
timber frame building, 29–30, 112, 114–15, 116
Todaiji monastery, Japan, 42
Toshodaiji Kondo, Japan, 42
tourism, 11–12, 13, 25, 52, 58
town, 12, 33, 49
Town and Country Planning Act, 1947, 152
town planning, 128, 130
townscape, 54
tradition, 17, 27, 29
trompe-l'oeil, 87, 89
Trucco, Matte, 122
Turkey, 40, 52, 147–8
Turner, John F. C., 149
TWA (John F. Kennedy) Terminal, New York, 133

Ungers, Matthias, 59, 139
Unité d'Habitation, Marseilles, 124
United States, 26, 27, 31, 32, 35–6, 50, 51, 55, 56, 58, 63, 68, 74, 78, 83, 115, 120, 121–2, 123, 124, 126, 128, 132, 134–5, 136, 140, 145, 152
Unwin, Raymond, 54
Ur, Chaldees, 33
urban design, 54, 64, 161
urban designers, 50, 54, 161
urban growth, 53, 146, 148, 149, 162
urbanism, 58
user participation, 96
'Usonia', 123
utopianism, 55
Utzon, Jorn, 133

Vanbrugh, Sir John, 11, 16, 44
Venice International Exhibition, 46
ventilation, 28
Venturi, Robert, 128, 133
vernacular architecture, 5, 26–36, 44, 50, 83, 120, 151, 152
vernacular technology, 30

INDEX

Vickers building, London, 85
Victorian style, 17, 21, 23–4
Vienna, 92
Vierzenheilegen pilgrimage church, Germany, 89
village, 33, 50
Villa Savoye, France, 123, 125
Ville Radieuse, 124
Vitruvius, 45, 78
Von Erlach, Fischer, 43
Vorkurs (Bauhaus course), 68

Wadham College, Oxford, 15
Wagner, Martin, 81
Warwick Castle, 86
wattle and daub, 30
'wealden type', 29–30
Webb, Philip, 119, 120
Wells Cathedral, Somerset, 88
Welwyn Garden City, 34
Westminster Abbey, London, 39
White, Stanford, 120
Wilford and Associates, Michael, 140
Wilkinson, W., 23

wind tunnel, 66
Wittgenstein, Ludwig, 152
Woburn Abbey, 11
Wolfson College, Oxford, 18
Woodward, Benjamin, 20
World Bank, 149
World Congress, 143, 144, 148
World War I, 34, 114–15
World War II, 115, 124, 126, 132, 138
Worringer, Wilhelm, 40
working class housing, 114, 128
working drawings, 70–1, 103
Wotton, Sir Henry, 78
Wren, Sir Christopher, 15, 16, 20, 44, 91, 157
Wright, Frank Lloyd, 94, 122, 123, 134
Wurzburg Residenz, Germany, 89
Wykeham, William of, 44

York Minster, 11

zeitgeist (spirit of the age), 53, 82
zoning, 54, 55, 130, 160